THE SON OF GOD

THE MYSTICAL TEACHINGS OF THE MASTERS

First Edition 1913
Reuben Swinburne Clymer

New Edition 2021
Edited by Tarl Warwick

THE SON OF GOD

COPYRIGHT AND DISCLAIMER

The first edition of this work is in the public domain having been written prior to 1926. This edition, with its cover art and format, is all rights reserved.

In no way may this text be construed as encouraging or condoning any harmful or illegal act. In no way may this text be construed as able to diagnose, treat, cure, or prevent any disease, injury, symptom, or condition.

THE SON OF GOD

FOREWORD

This book is technically an interpretation of Christianity according to the professed illuminati of Swinburne Clymer, stressing the mystical and initially Essene origin of Jesus Christ and his teachings, deviated from the practices of the Sadducees, Pharisees, and other more mainstream Judaist groups of antiquity contemporary to the first century CE. Much of the content deals with divine law- especially nonviolence, self control and self awareness, and related themes. As with most works by this author, it combines Eastern and Western spiritual practice- which makes sense if one interprets Jesus as having been predominantly concerned with a form of unorthodox mysticism.

The essential topic here is evinced by biblical passages which do indeed (as interpreted) provide evidence for Jesus not having been involved with the variously political and materialistic religious norms of his purported time of life. This principle is still widely taught today, within and without the circles of the occult.

This edition of "The Son of God" has been carefully edited for format and content. Care has been taken to retain all original intent and meaning.

THE SON OF GOD

FOREWORD

Among the foremost teachers that America ever had, stood Dr. James R. Phelps, he who is now passed to the Beyond.

Not only on account of his learning, his knowledge of the dead languages and of the Ancient Teachings, but also on account of his absolute honesty and sincerity was he one of the foremost teachers.

In a letter, which he invariably wrote to the beginner who came under his training, he said:

"My authority- and I dislike that word- goes back for years, and was conferred by honored brothers now resting from their labors. For reasons of my own, when I affiliated with the Order Illuminati- of which Count Giounotti, (then here he mentions the names by which the Master is known,) was the Hierophant- I doubted my ability to take any prominent position in its activities, and they assigned me to the care of the back door, to take charge of those who, fainting by the way or discouraged by the apparent obstacles in the way, were giving up in despair. They called me '___' or 'the Keeper of the Door.' I found out in time that there was but one door to The Temple, and that entrance and exit were the same. Our Master says: 'I am the door, by it any man enter in he shall be safe, and go in and go out, and shall find pasture.' Now, my dear brother, divert yourself of any idea you may have that my position confers on me any superiority over you. That is the rock on which many a pseudo teacher has gone to pieces. 'Call no man your Master on earth, for One is your Master, the Christ, and all ye are brethren.'"

This will show more clearly than any words of mine as to

THE SON OF GOD

the worth of this grand teacher. No man would he allow to call him Master; but the student might call him Teacher or Guide. And this was the man from whom I received much of my training and from whom I learned much of the Sublime Mysteries concerning the Soul and its Powers.

In my interpretation I therefore come to you with knowledge received through a training of nearly eighteen years, much of which was under men who claimed nothing for themselves except that they were laborers in the vineyard of the Master and desired no praise, but desired that all praise should be given to the Master.

Brotherly Given,

The Author.

THE SON OF GOD

PREFACE

A. Reville, the French writer, sizing up the religious feeling of his time, wrote to this effect: "Always in all human societies, at a certain period of their existence, a time comes when their religion begins to diverge from its fundamental meaning, then diverges more and more, loses this fundamental meaning, and finally crystallizes into permanently established forms. When it does so, its influence upon the life of men grows weaker and weaker as it becomes more of a form from which the life has departed. At such periods, the educated minority, though no longer believing in the existing religious teaching, still pretend to believe, finding this religion necessary for holding the masses in the established order of life; whilst the masses, although adhering by the force of inertia to the established religious forms, are no longer guided in their lives by religious demands, but only by popular customs and laws. So it has been, many times, in many human communities. But what is now taking place in our Christian society has never occurred before. The ruling and more educated minority, which has the chief influence on the masses, not only disbelieves in the existing religion, but is certain that religion is no longer necessary at all. It teaches those who doubt the truth of the accepted faith not some other more rational and comprehensive religion than that existing, but persuades them that religion in general has outlived its time, and has become not only a useless but even a harmful organ of social life. Religion is studied by this class of men not as something which we know through our inner experience, but as an external phenomenon, a ritual of mere fancy words, a disease, as it were, to which some people are subject, and which we can understand only in its external symptoms. It is because religion is thus considered that so very many have come to believe in nothing."

"Religion remains, as it always was, the chief motive power, the heart of the life of human societies. Without it, as

THE SON OF GOD

without the heart, there can be no rational life. There have been, and there are, many different religions, because the expression of the relation of man to the Infinite, to God, or the gods, is different at different times, according to the different degrees of development of different nations; but no society of men, since men have become rational beings, could ever live, and therefore never did live, without religion. It is true that there have been, and still occur, periods in the life of nations when the existing religion was so distorted and so far behind life that it no longer guided man, and such a period is the present one. But this cessation of the influence of religion, has been only temporary. Religion, like everything vital, has the capacity of being born, developing, growing old, and dying, of reviving again, and reviving again in a more perfect form than ever before. After the period of the highest development of religion there always follows a period of weakness and lifelessness, after which again there generally follows a period of regeneration, or new interpretation, and of the establishment of a religious teaching more clear and rational than before. Such periods of development, decline, and regeneration have occurred in all religions; and such a period is there now. Religion, in fact, is the definition of man's life by the connection of the human with the Divine, the power of which over the universe and himself he recognizes and with which he feels that he must unite himself and come into conscious relationship."

Each age demands a distinctive type of interpretation of truth, adapted to the requirements of that particular period of history. (The following paragraphs are practically verbatim extracts from "The Fundamental Principles of the Church of Illumination," which appeared in The Initiates of November, 1912.) Truth is ever the same. Divine laws have not changed since the beginning of time. But the world of thought advances; and each outgoing cycle requires a laying aside of its cloak, as the snake sheds its skin, that the incoming cycle may be "clothed upon" with a new garment, better suited to its needs. The texture and the designs and the coloring of the cloak of thought are

THE SON OF GOD

determined by the particular emphasis that a given age employs in the interpretation of truth. For the human race to be enriched by all the varied aspects that truth and its realization may assume, it is necessary for the cloak of interpretation to be doffed and donned, again and again, in accordance with the laws of progress; it is necessary for a new system of emphasis in the interpretation of truth to be formulated from time to time.

The doffing of an old interpretation and the donning of a new marks a transition period that is attended by unsettledness of mind and by perplexity of thought. It is truly a period of stress and strain. The world of religious ideas is now in a transitional stage. To satisfy this need, the Temple of Illumination, of which this little volume is a text-book, offers a new system of interpretation- an interpretation that claims to be the natural outgrowth of the cyclic stage through which the world has already passed, and it furthermore claims to be the highest interpretation that can be given to truth, because it goes at once to the base and the ultimate of all that is- the Soul of man.

The law of cyclic changes indicates that the time is ripe for a re-statement of religious principles, for a new presentation of fundamental laws. The unrest and the hunger of the present transitional stage of thought demands a different placing of emphasis in respect to the essential features of truth.

When interpreted in the light of symbology, the Bible is accepted by the Temple of Illumination as an authoritative treatise of religious instruction; but, in order to secure a satisfactory comprehension of Biblical teachings, it is deemed necessary to give careful attention to its symbolic, allegorical, and mystic elements. The interpreter must learn to consult the vast library of legend and symbol and myth as faithfully and as accurately as he resorts to a lexicon of Hebrew and Greek stems and radicals; for such elements as these, sometimes considered mere meaningless child's play, are skillful devices for half-concealing, yet half-

THE SON OF GOD

revealing, the deepest spiritual truths.

The religious thought of the past centuries has been largely characterized by faith and belief. In respect to the teachings of Jesus, the Christ of the first century, the race-conception of truth has been passing through the period of childhood and early youth. Childhood is marked particularly by faith. The child has faith in his father. The child believes in his father's works and in his principles. When young manhood is attained, he is no longer satisfied with mere belief; he must demonstrate his faith by executing ideals; he must do such works as his father does. As a young man, he still has faith in his father; but his faith now demands the opportunity to exercise its own powers and to accomplish its own works. Religious teaching in the past has been largely occupied in the effort to convince mankind of the Messiahship of Jesus, and to establish the claims of the Christ. But mere faith does not long satisfy. "Faith without works is dead," is something more than a trite saying. It is a law of growth that faith must demonstrate its powers; it must work out its principles; it must execute; it must create. The incoming age should be one that is characterized by the power of intelligent faith, one that executes ideals in harmony with a faith that understands divine law.

A clear distinction should be made between blind faith and intelligent, or a seeing, faith; between faith that is passive and one that is active; between an inert and a living faith; between faith in a personality and faith in a principle, faith in a Jesus and faith in the Christ. Jesus is the name of a man, a personality. The Christ is the name of the Conscious Individualized Illuminated Soul of Jesus. Jesus, as an historic character, lived his earth-life, and passed out of the plane of manifestation. The Christ, as a divine principle developed and individualized in Jesus, is eternal; as an Illuminated Soul, the Christ is immortal. Faith in Jesus, as a personality merely, is a blind faith. Faith in the Christ, as a state of consciousness that all may attain by living the teachings of Jesus and by obeying the law of love he demonstrated, is an intelligent, an active faith.

How was Jesus enabled to live the perfect life- a life the entire biography of which may be condensed into five words: "He went about doing good?" To many, these answers will be convincing: by an intelligent obedience to divine law; by a conscious realization of truth, by the transmuting power of goodness; by a conscious application of the never-failing law of love and good-will to men; by a masterful directing of a purified will, by a faith that consciously operates in harmony with divine law; by the unconscious influence of a thought-atmosphere, normally characterized by the qualities of love, truth, and justice; by an illumination of Soul that radiates its own light of understanding and its own warmth of love, on friend and foe, with impartial tenderness; by a prayer-life that attracts, from the infinite storehouse, a supply equal to its own demands. The many who are satisfied with such answers as these are ready for a change of emphasis in the interpretation of the life and the teachings of Jesus. The many already are thoroughly convinced of the genuineness, the sincerity, and the truth of his claim to be the Son of Man and the Son of God. Such as these are eager for emphasis to be placed on the interpretation of the law that enabled him to realize His divine Sonship, and, in consequence, to live such a life. They are eager to understand "the way, the truth, and the life," that will enable them to become conscious of Sonship with the Father, and thus to live the good life. Their faith refuses to be satisfied unless it can express itself in works that exemplify its character. Their natures demand a fulfillment of the age of faith by an age of works that test and prove the law of faith, as lived by Jesus, the Master. Their natures demand a proof of the Christie teachings in their own experience, a verification of the Christie law in their own consciousness. Such a faith manifests itself by a willingness to put forth every effort to understand the law of the Christ, and by a determination to obey this law in their own lives.

THE SON OF GOD

To meet the need of the age in its demand for an interpretation of the laws of the kingdom of the Soul, is one purpose of this book as it is of the Temple of Illumination. That it is possible for man to understand, and that it is necessary for him to understand in order that he may intelligently obey the law and live a life in harmony with it, is a settled conviction among leaders of religious thought today.

That immortality of soul is attainable, is a fundamental doctrine of the Temple of Illumination. Immortality of soul, however, is not thought of as something that is thrust on all alike, regardless of their desire or their seeking. It is not an inevitable factor of existence. The positive law of goodness functioning in the lives of men leads to immortality of soul, or to Soul Consciousness. In each life is a spark, or a germ, of the divine nature. This divine spark is the potential Christ, or the potential individual soul, of that life. This may be nurtured and fed until it becomes "the light that lighteth all the world" of man's consciousness. When man becomes conscious of this Light within his own being, when he recognizes and obeys its "still, small voice," he has reached the state called Illumination of Soul, or Immortality; or, to express the same thought differently, he has reached the plane of Soul Consciousness.

The divine spark latent in each individual may become a well-formed center of pure, white light. It may become a dynamic nucleus of fire- the Fire of Love, the Light of Truth. This fact gives the key to the significance of the name, Temple of Illumination. The name signifies that each individual is capable of becoming a center of illumination. Man is the Temple of Illumination, the Temple of the living Christ. Man is the architect of the temple of Solomon, which is a spiritual structure. The purified love of his own heart and the clarified understanding of his own soul become the altar-fire of this temple. This flame unconsciously radiates its light of understanding and its warmth of "good- will toward men."

THE SON OF GOD

Man is made in the image of God. He is a reflection of the Divine, possessing the powers and the attributes of the Infinite. In different beings, these divine qualities are in different stages of unfoldment. In one, they may be in a latent state, concealed from view beneath the crust of a selfish personality; but, unless they have been burned and seared by the fire of persistent wrong-doing, they are none the less a potentiality, awaiting the unfolding processes of growth. In another, they may be in the incipient stages of a nucleus of goodness. In this state, they indicate an active, wholesome conscience; although the life may be painfully entangled and fettered and hampered by the lower personality. Yet, again, these qualities may have become a dynamic, vital expression of individualized life, such that the soul is conscious of its inseparable connection with the Infinite. They may have condensed into a center of radiation, into a perfect, pyramidal flame that warms the desire-nature with love, and illumines the understanding with truth. In this state, the divine qualities of love, truth, and justice unconsciously radiate, to those with whom the life comes in contact, the blessings of their inherent goodness.

Creation is the manifestation of the Divine Mind. All things, having been created by God, are, in themselves, good; but, through free-will, man may pervert the good by wrong use, and thus cause evil; he may misdirect possibilities that are inherently blessed, and thus bring on himself and others a painful curse.

In his fourfold nature, body, mind, spirit, and soul, man is an epitome of the universe. Potentially, he is the divine creation in miniature, and, consequently, has been called the microcosm, or "little world." He is the climax and culmination of forces, which for ages have been seeking expression. How to use his forces and to express them harmoniously, is the problem placed before him. To use them in harmony with the divine purpose and to express them only in service to mankind- this is the ideal he must be led to understand and to choose for himself. To use his powers and his possibilities in obedience to the law of goodness and in keeping

THE SON OF GOD

with the correct understanding of truth, leads to good. To pervert his powers and to misdirect his inherent possibilities in channels of error and sin, result in evil.

God has placed no higher mark of honor on man than to give him the right of choice, the power of decision, and the ability to direct will-power and to execute plans in accordance with his own decree. Every power is, in itself, good, although it admits of a twofold expression, positive and negative. Every law of his nature is, in itself, good, although it admits of a twofold functioning, constructive and upbuilding or destructive and disintegrating. The use one makes of a law determines its effect. Every virtue admits of a corresponding vice. Results depend on the use given to power, on the direction that a tendency takes. Every force, every possibility placed within man's reach, is intended to fulfill certain beneficent ends. Every organ, every function, both of body and of mind, is intended to serve a certain noble purpose. When used in harmony with the law of its highest purpose, the result is good. It is time for man to understand that he is individually responsible for putting forth intelligent effort to understand the laws of his own being and to obey their highest call.

One distinctive aim of this book, as it is of the Temple of Illumination, is to give clear instructions concerning the laws of right and justice in order that man may intelligently choose his steps, and know how to cultivate his manifold powers and to direct them in proper channels. The Christie Law is the law of growth, advancement, and progress. Both in its positive and in its negative aspects, this law is exacting and relentless. Obedience to it is constructive and upbuilding, and tends toward growth of soul, reaching as its natural goal the plane of Soul Consciousness, or immortality of soul. Failure to comply with the conditions of the Christie Law is destructive and disintegrating in its effects. It tends toward diffusion and dissolution. Its results are the opposite of growth; namely, self-destruction and continual tearing down of cells. The Temple of Illumination is pronounced in its recognition

THE SON OF GOD

of this law, both in its positive and in its negative aspects. Consequently, while it continually holds before the mind the ideal of growth and development that lead to immortality of soul, yet it admits that persistent evil thinking and evil doing tend toward total destruction of soul. To create and to follow evil persistently, by the operation of its own law, generates the fire that is self-destructive, and thus makes possible the dissolution of the individual soul that creates such disintegrating conditions, thereby liberating the original element of potential divinity.

The positive work of the law of the Christ is known as the process of salvation, or regeneration; while, in its negative working, it is called degeneration, or loss, of soul. The doctrine of salvation, or regeneration, receives practical attention in the teachings of the Temple of Illumination; but, as a dogma or definition of terms, the doctrine offers little interest. Salvation does not specify a definite act, but a long-continued process of growth, or development, of soul. It results in illumination of soul, or immortality, or soul consciousness. These, in turn, are stages of growth, and are not to be thought of as a climax of perfection that ends all effort, struggle, and attainment. Illumination of soul is but the beginning of thought and experience on a higher plane of expression.

The chief reason for the Christie teaching is the establishment of direct communication or communion between God and man. Every man who takes upon himself the role of intercessor in this communion hinders those he wishes to guide, from entering into direct communion with God through the means of their own Conscious Individualized Soul. All that the teacher can do is to point the way. Man himself must travel the path that leads to Divine Illumination.

The book now before the reader attempts to do this. It attempts to give a clear, positive interpretation of the teachings as given to mankind by Jesus- an interpretation, which, if lived and

THE SON OF GOD

not merely believed in, will help those so living to reach illumination of soul.

"By what sign shall I overcome the powers of the earth?"

The Within: "By the sign of the Son of Man."

"Show thou me this sign."

THE SON OF GOD

JESUS AS AN ESSENE

At the time of the birth of Jesus, there were three orders among the Jews. They were very similar in their organization; hut there was a wide difference in their teachings. These sects or organizations were the Pharisees, the Sadducees, and the Essenes. We will first speak of the Pharisees and the Sadducees.

Both the Pharisees and the Sadducees were cordially united in sentiment respecting all those fundamental points which constituted the basis of the Jewish religion. All of them rejected with detestation the notion of a plurality of gods. They acknowledged the existence of but one Almighty God, or Power, whom they regarded as the Creator of the Universe, and whom they believed to be endowed with the most absolute perfection. In this belief, the Essenes also shared. Both sects were equally agreed in the opinion that God had selected the Hebrews from among all other nations of the earth as His peculiar people, and had bound them to Himself by an unchangeable and everlasting covenant. With the same unanimity they maintained the divine mission of Moses; that he was the ambassador of heaven; and, consequently, that the law delivered at Mount Sinai and promulgated by his ministry was of divine origin. It was also the general belief among both sects, that in the books of the Old Testament were contained ample instructions respecting the way of salvation and eternal happiness; and that whatever principles or duties were inculcated in those writings must be reverently received and implicitly obeyed.

But an almost irreconcilable difference of opinion, and the most vehement disputes prevailed among them, respecting the original source, or fountain, whence all religion was to be deduced. The Sadducees rejected with disdain the oral law, to which the Pharisees paid the greatest deference. And the interpretation of the written law yielded still further ground for acrimonious contention. The Pharisees maintained that the law as committed to writing by Moses, and likewise every other part of the sacred volumes had a twofold sense, or meaning: the one plain and obvious to every reader, and the other abstruse and mystical. This was also a fundamental belief of the Essenes, and is, to this day, of the successors of the Essenes- the Rosicrucian Fraternity. The Sadducees, on the contrary, would admit of nothing beyond a simple interpretation of the words according to their strict literal sense. The Essenes, however, differed somewhat from both in this: first, they considered the words of the law to possess no force or power whatever in themselves, but merely to exhibit the shadows or the images of celestial objects, of virtues, and of duties; second, they regarded that salvation could not come by mere faith in the law, but by doing as the law commanded.

In point of number, riches, authority, and influence, the Pharisees took precedence of all Jewish sects. And as they constantly manifested an extraordinary display of religion, in an apparent zeal for the cultivation of piety and brotherly love, and by an affectation of superior sanctity in their opinions, manners, and dress, the influence which they possessed over the minds of the people was unbounded; insomuch that it may almost be said that they gave whatever direction they pleased to public affairs. It is unquestionable, however, that the religion of the Pharisees for the most part was founded in consummate hypocrisy; and that in reality they were generally the slaves of every vicious appetite; proud, arrogant, and avaricious, consulting only the gratification of their lusts, even at the moment of their professing to be engaged in the service of their Maker. These odious features in the character of the Pharisees drew upon them the most pointed rebukes from Jesus; with more severity indeed than he bestowed on the Sadducees, who, although they had departed widely from the genuine principles of religion, yet did not impose themselves upon mankind by a pretended sanctity or devote themselves with insatiable greediness to the acquisition of honors and riches. The Pharisees admitted the immortality of the soul, the resurrection of the body, and a future state of rewards and punishments. They admitted, to a certain extent, the free agency of man; but, beyond that, they supposed his actions to be controlled by the decree of fate. These points of doctrine, however, seem not to have been understood or explained by the sects in the same way, neither does it appear that either of the two took any great pains to define and to ascertain them with accuracy and precision or to support them by reasoning and argument.

The Sadducees were a sect much inferior in point of number to that of the Pharisees, but composed entirely of persons distinguished for their opulence and prosperity. Those who belonged to them were wholly devoid of the sentiments of benevolence and compassion towards others; whereas, the Pharisees, according to authority, were ever ready to relieve the wants of the needy and the afflicted. The Sadducees were fond of passing their lives in one uninterrupted course of ease and pleasure; insomuch that it was with difficulty they could be prevailed on to undertake the duties of the magistracy or any other public function. Their leading tenet was that all our hopes and fears terminate with the present life, the soul being involved in one common fate with the body, and, like it, liable to perish and be annihilated.

Upon this principle, it was natural for the Sadducees to maintain that obedience to the Divine Law would be rewarded by the Most High with length of days and an abundance of the good things of this life, such as honors, distinctions, and riches; while the violators of it, in like manner, would find their punishment in the temporary sufferings and afflictions of the present time. Therefore, they always connected the favor of heaven with a state of worldly prosperity, and could not regard any as virtuous, or the friends of heaven, except the fortunate and the happy; they had no bowels of compassion for the poor and the miserable; their desires and hopes centered in a life of pleasure, leisure, ease, and voluptuous gratifications. This is precisely the character that

THE SON OF GOD

reliable authority gives them. Also, this idea appears to be countenanced by the sacred writings- especially if, as is now generally admitted, the master Jesus, in the parable of the rich man and Lazarus, designed, in the person of the former, to delineate the principles and manners of life of a Sadducee.

Although not mentioned openly in the Bible for the reason that Jesus was one of them, the Essenes existed as a sect in the time of Jesus and were divided into two branches: the one was characterized by a life of celibacy, dedicated to the instruction and education of the children of others; while the other branch- the Therapeutae- thought it proper to marry, not with a view of sensual gratification, but for the purpose of propagating the human species, and for the purpose of the development of a certain power which is possible only through the rites of true marriage. Hence, they were distinguished by the people as the practical and the theoretical Essenes.

The Essenes were distributed in the cities and throughout the countries of Syria, Palestine, and Egypt. In fact, they were the natural successors to the Egyptian Initiates after the fall of the temples of Initiation in Egypt. Their bond of association embraced not merely a community of tenets and similarity of manners and particular observances, but it extended also to an intercommunity of goods. Their demeanor was sober and chaste; and their mode of life, in every respect, was subjected to the strictest regulations and was submitted to the superintendence of governors, whom they appointed over themselves and who held such position for life. In like manner, the governor, now known as the Grand Master, is at the head of the Rosicrucian Fraternity, in each country, for life.

The whole of their time was devoted to labor, meditation, and prayer; and they were most sedulously attentive to the calls of justice and humanity, and of every moral duty. They believed in the unity of God, or the one Supreme Being, with principalities and hierarchies less than the One Supreme God. They believed the

THE SON OF GOD

soul to have fallen, through disobedience to the Divine Law, from the regions of purity and light into the dark bodies which men occupy as the house of the soul; they considered men, during their continuance in the body, to be confined, as it were, within the wall of loathsome prisons which had to be changed into the temples of God through obedience to the Divine Law. They cultivated great abstinence, allowing themselves but little bodily nourishment or gratification, The ceremonies and rituals, or external forms, which were enjoined by the laws of Moses to be observed in the worship of God, were not regarded by the Essenes as necessary except as symbolizing the greater worship within the temple of man. Like the old Initiates of Egypt, they held that the Ritualistic form or ceremony should not be held by the neophytes until after they had first manifested an interior Initiation. The experience of Initiation the Temple of the Illuminati calls Individualized Soul Consciousness, and the Rosicrucian Fraternity calls it "Passing the Threshold."

This same form is today observed by the Rosicrucian Fraternity, as also by the Temple of the Illuminati, which is the outer court of the Rosicrucian Fraternity, as was the Therapeutae, an outer circle of the Essenes. No neophyte can take part in the ceremonial ritual until, through training, not mere study, he has passed the Threshold and has found the Christ, or reached Soul Consciousness. In accordance with the teachings of the Essenes, of Jesus and of the Rosicrucian Fraternity, even this ceremonial initiation is not actually required; but it helps to bind its Initiates into a closer bond of Brotherhood in that it brings them together in symbolizing outwardly that which they have already found within themselves.

Only sacrifices of incense were offered by the Essenes; but this they did in their homes.

Although Jesus often denounced both the Pharisees and the Sadducees most bitterly, there is not a single instance of his

THE SON OF GOD

having anything to say against the Essenes; and this alone is evidence that, even if he had not been one of them, he must have agreed with their doctrine and have found nothing against them. But there is manuscript proof in abundance that he received his whole training in their temples both in Palestine and in Egypt.

In all points, the teachings of the Essenes exactly corresponded to what Jesus taught during his ministry and to much of what is now being taught by their successors- the Rosicrucian Fraternity and its outer courts. Both teach a selfless, purified life- a life of love, cheer, and ministry among all humanity. Their abstinence from all harmful things that the world and the flesh adhere to, love and teach, proves that they understood the illusions of these human beliefs and teachings, and their inadequacy for happiness and for the development that leads to life eternal. Jesus did not desire what the world offered him, "he was tempted in all points like as we are;" but he understood. To understand is to know. Jesus understood the Law, for he had been fully taught it. In temptation, he understood that the claims and offers were false and evil, that they offered only temporary benefits, and did not lead to Divine Truth and Unity. Wisdom is not knowledge of books nor yet of any teachings. "Wisdom is understanding through becoming.

When the soul unfolds and develops into the vibration and the currents that constitute Soul Wisdom, or God's Wisdom, we know that what evil claims as goodness or knowledge, wisdom and happiness, is not really such; and we know that there cannot be anything desirable in or through evil. There is only one way to attain Soul Wisdom, and that is to turn away from false beliefs.

All men should know, all religions should teach, that the One God, the God of the Egyptians, the God of Moses, of Abraham, Isaac, and Jacob, and the God of Jesus is the Creator, the Controller, the Ruler, of the Universe. All admit that God is Omnipotent, Universal, and Divine. All admit that God rules, is

THE SON OF GOD

immutable, and Supreme. Yet very few are willing to be like Him, to do like Him, and thereby to become like Him, the Sons of God.

All admit that to attain Sonship with Him, to know Him, to become like Him, we must be like Him. We must be "raised up in His likeness." The mortal must be changed, transmuted; it must put on Immortality. The corruptible must put on incorruption. In putting on incorruption, it is not necessary to lay aside the material body; for the material is changeable, not merely at death, but also during life; and it is indeed for the very purpose of making this change that man is on the earth plane and has the earthly, or carnal, body.

This mystery of transmutation Jesus had been taught. More than this, he had to live the life among the Essenes that brought about such a change. In all his teachings he taught this doctrine, and how to accomplish the change from corruptible to incorruptible. This was the purpose of his ministry.

God is Intelligence. He is Universal Intelligence and Wisdom. This Universal Intelligence is in all things. "All that was, was made by Him." Without this Wisdom and Intelligence can nothing be made, for God is in all things. The Infinite Wisdom is all that is, all that has been, and all that ever will be. If the Universal Intelligence controls all things, and is changeless, then immortal man, made in His image, is like Him. He has wisdom and intelligence, and is empowered even with means of access to the Divine Intelligence and Wisdom. This is the stage of consciousness that Jesus attained through the training he received from the Essenes. He attained it through the awakening and the development of the Soul.

As man lays aside, or draws away from, all that the world offers, all that the carnal man seeks to attain in ambition, fame, self-glory, he is able to grow into the full realization of his Divine Being, and to attain far more than the world can ever give him.

THE SON OF GOD

Soul Development, or spiritual training, alone is the key to the door of wisdom and knowledge. The Essenes trained and developed the boy Jesus into the great and wonderful Christ. Development is not only controlling and subduing the physical and the material, but it is also the process of bringing into life the divine spark within man. As this is awakened and aroused to consciousness, there is a gain of wisdom; for the Awakened Soul is in communion with the Father who knows all things and who gives all knowledge to those that are like Him.

"Jesus (The following paragraphs are taken verbatim from Jesus, the last great Initiate, by E. Shure (pp. 25 ff.). What appears in brackets is the comment of the author of this book) passed his early years amid the calm of Galilee. His first impressions were gentle, austere, and serene. His birthplace resembled a corner of heaven, dropped on the side of a mountain. The village of Nazareth has changed but little with the flight of time. Its houses, rising in tiers under the rock, resembled white cubes scattered about in a forest of pomegranate, vine, and fig trees, whilst myriads of doves filled the heavens. Around this nest of verdant freshness floats the pure mountain air, whilst on the heights may be seen the open, clear horizon of Galilee. Add to this imposing background the quiet, solemn home-life of a pious, patriarchal family. The strength of Jewish education lay always in the unity of law and faith, as well as in the powerful organization of the family dominated by the national and religious idea. The paternal home was a kind of temple for the child... The union of father and mother in mutual love of their children illumined and warmed the house with a distinctly spiritual life. It was there Jesus received his early instruction, and first became acquainted with the scriptures under the teachings of his parents. (There is evidence that his mother only was capable of instructing him.) From his earliest childhood the long strange destiny of the people of God appeared before him in the periodic feasts and holy days celebrated in family life by reading, song, and prayer. At the Feast of Tabernacles, a shed, made of myrtle and olive branches, was

THE SON OF GOD

erected in the court or on the roof of the house in memory of the nomad patriarchs of bygone days. The seven-branched candlestick was lit, and there were produced the rolls of papyrus from which the secret history was read aloud. To the child's mind, the Eternal was present, not merely in the starry sky, but even in this candlestick, the reflex of his glory, in the speech of the father and the silent love of the mother. Thus Jesus was made acquainted with the great days in Israel's history, days of joy and sorrow, of triumph and exile, of numberless afflictions and eternal hope. The father gave no reply to the child's eager and direct questions. But the mother (having received much of the Mystic training from the Essenes) said to him: 'The Word of God lives in his prophets alone. Some day the wise Essenes, solitary wanderers by Mount Carmel and the Dead Sea, will give thee an answer.' However powerful might have been the impressions of the outer world on the Soul of Jesus, they all grew pale before the sovereign and inexpressible truth in his inner world. This truth was expanding in the depths of his nature, like some lovely flower emerging from a dark pool. It resembled a growing light which appeared to him when alone in silent meditation. At such times, men and things, whether near or far away, appeared as though transparent in their essence. He read thoughts and saw souls; then, in memory, he caught glimpses, as though through a thin veil, of divinely beautiful and shining beings bending over him, or assembled in adoration of a dazzling light. (For the hierarchies were ever near him and guiding him.) Wonderful visions came in his sleep, or interposed themselves between himself and reality by a veritable duplication of his consciousness. In these transports of rapture which carried him from zone to zone as though towards other skies, he at times felt himself attracted by a mighty dazzling light, and then plunged into an incandescent sun. These ravishing experiences left behind in him a spring of ineffable tenderness, a source of wonderful strength. How perfect was the reconciliation he felt with all beings, in what sublime harmony was he with the universe! But what was this mysterious light- though even more familiar and living than the other- which sprang forth from the

THE SON OF GOD

depths of his nature, carrying him away to the most distant tracts of space, and yet uniting him by secret vibrations with all souls? Was it not the source of souls and worlds? (Was it not his own soul having become awakened and Conscious? For all those who follow the Path see the same dazzling light and are enveloped in and by it.)"

"He named it His Father in heaven. This primitive feeling of unity with God in the light of Love is the first, the great revelation to Jesus. An inner voice told him to hide it deep in his heart; all the same, it was to give light to his whole life. It gave him an invincible feeling of certainty, made him at once gentle and indomitable; converted his thoughts into a diamond shield, and his speech into a sword of flame. Besides, this profoundly secret, mystical life was united with a perfect clearness in matters of every-day life. Luke shows him at the age of twelve years as 'increasing in strength, grace, and wisdom.' The religious consciousness was, in Jesus, innate, absolutely independent of the outer world. His prophetic and Messianic consciousness could only be awakened by outer circumstances, by the life of his age, in short, by special initiation and long elaboration. (Through his early teachings, through soul training, and through self-mastery in thought, desire, and deed.) Traces of this are found in the Gospels and elsewhere. The first great shock came to him during a journey to Jerusalem with his parents, as related by Luke. This town, the pride of Israel, had become the center of Jewish aspirations. Its misfortunes had had no other effect than to exalt the minds of men. Under the Seleucides and Maccabees, first by Pompey and finally by Herod, Jerusalem had been subjected to the most terrible of sieges. Blood had been shed in torrents; the Roman legions had butchered the people in its streets, and innumerable crucifixions had polluted the surrounding heights. After such horrors, and the humiliation following on the Roman occupation, after decimating the Sanhedrim and reducing the pontiff to a mere trembling slave, Herod, as though in irony, had rebuilt the temple with more magnificent pomp and glory than ever. Jerusalem remained, as

THE SON OF GOD

before, the holy city. Had not Isaiah, the favorite author of Jesus, named it 'the Bride, before whom the people shall bow down'? He had said: 'The Gentiles shall come to thy light, and kings to the brightness of thy rising... Violence shall no more be heard in thy land, wasting nor destruction within thy borders; but thou shalt call thy walls Salvation and thy gates Peace.' To see Jerusalem and the temple of Jehovah was the dream of all Jews, especially since Judea had become a Roman province. They journeyed hither from Perea, Galilee, Alexandria, and Babylon. On the way, whether in the wilderness under the waving palms, or near the wells, they cast longing eyes, as they sang their psalms, in the direction of the hill of Zion. A strange feeling of oppression must have come over the soul of Jesus, when, on his first pilgrimage, he saw the city girt around with lofty walls, standing there on the mountain, like a gloomy fortress, the Roman amphitheater of Herod at its gates, the Antonia tower dominating the temple, and Roman legions- lance in hand- keeping watch from the heights. He ascended the temple steps, and admired the beauty of those marble porticoes, along which walked the Pharisees in sumptuous flowing robes. (The Pharisees whom he was later so bitterly to denounce!)"

"After crossing the Gentiles', he proceeded to the women's court, and, mingling with the crowd of Israelites, drew near the Nicanor gate, and the three-cubit balustrade, behind which were to be seen priests in sacerdotal robes of purple and violet, shining with gold and precious stones, officiating there in front of the sanctuary, sacrificing bulls and goats, and sprinkling the blood over the people as they pronounced a blessing. All this bore no resemblance to the temple of his dreams, or the heaven in his heart. (The temple of his dreams was the temple of his own soul, revealed to him by the Inner Consciousness of God within his own being.) Then he descended again into the more populous quarters of the town, where he saw beggars pallid with hunger, and whose faces were torn with anguish; a veritable reflection of the tortures and crucifixions accompanying the late wars. Leaving the city by one of the gates, he wandered among those stony valleys and

THE SON OF GOD

gloomy ravines forming the quarries, pools, and tombs of the kings, and converting Jerusalem into a veritable sepulcher. There he saw maniacs issue from the caves, shrieking out blasphemies against living and dead alike. Then, descending a broad flight of stones to the pool of Siloam, he saw stretched out at the water's brink lepers, paralytics, and wretches, covered with ulcers and sores, in the most abject misery. An irresistible impulse compelled him to look deep into their eyes, and drink in all their grief and pain. (As must do all those who would be saviors of their race.) Some asked him for help, others were gloomy and hopeless, others again, with senses numbed, seemed to have done with suffering. Then Jesus said to himself: 'Of what use are these priests, this temple and these sacrifices, since they can afford no relief to this terrible suffering?' And, of a sudden, like an overwhelming torrent, he felt pouring into his heart the grief and pain of this town and its inhabitants- of the whole of humanity. He understood now that a happiness he could not share with others was absolutely impossible. These looks of despair were never more to leave his memory. Human suffering, a sad-faced bride, would henceforth accompany him everywhere, whispering in his ear: 'I will never leave thee more.' His soul full of anguish, he left Jerusalem, and proceeded towards the open peaks of Galilee. A cry leapt forth from the depths of his heart: 'Father in heaven! Grant that I may know, and heal, and save.'"

This mighty prayer that went forth from the heart of Jesus could be granted by none other than the Essenes; for they alone, in that vast country, could teach him. Neither the Pharisees nor the Sadducees claimed to know, to heal, or to save. The Essenes alone gave their whole time and their whole life to the work of teaching humanity, of healing them, and of trying to teach them how to save themselves; for it is a fundamental doctrine that man must save himself through the awakening of his inner consciousness, or the finding of the Christ.

Thus, at the age of thirteen years, Jesus entered the

THE SON OF GOD

Essenian school, as had his mother before him. Of the teachings we can bring to the attention of the reader those which were not secret; but of his training nothing may be said. For that was as secret at that day as it is at the present; and only those who are willing to know, to heal, and to save humanity can receive such a training.

The student reader may think this purely conjecture, but it is not. For the older manuscripts are before us, which contain the undeniable record of such training or initiation, and, so far as the world is concerned, we need but ask: Why did not Jesus attack with his unparalleled courage the Essenes as he did all the other religious sects of his day? Why did he not even mention them except in so far as their doctrines are concerned? Why did not the other apostles speak of them and denounce them? All of them knew that such a religious sect as the Essenes existed and that they were a mighty band. For only one reason: both Jesus and John had been taught by the Order, and they both were teaching much to the people that had before been taught only to the Inner Circle because the people were not yet ready to receive the truth.

In the time of Jesus, the order of the Essenes constituted the last remnant of brotherhoods which were established by the Egyptian Priests and by the later prophets. It was no new order; for, in its earlier times, the same teachings were expounded in Atlantis. It was simply a re-institution of a brotherhood as old as conscious humanity. The despotism of the rulers of all countries at that time, the jealousy of an ambitious and imbecile priesthood, had forced the order to take refuge in silence and solitude. They did not struggle as did those who went before them, but contentedly devoted themselves to preserving their traditions and their sublime teachings and training for such few as voluntarily came to them for that purpose.

They had a number of principal centers: one in Egypt, on the banks of the Lake Maoris; one in Palestine at Engaddi, near the

THE SON OF GOD

Dead Sea; and the others secret. The name of Essenes was no doubt derived from the Syrian word "Asaya," a physician- in Greek, therapeutes. But this word had also another meaning, it meant a teacher; and the two words, teacher and physician, made the third- a saver of mankind. For this they were, healers, teachers, and savers of mankind. Their only work, in so far as the people were concerned, was that of healing both the physical and the moral diseases of mankind. As to themselves, they worked as hard as any man could; and all the food that they required was raised by themselves. A part of their time was given to training- prayer, study, exercises, et cetera; another part, to humanity; and another, to physical labor.

Some of them, as in the present time with the true Initiates, were possessed of the gift of prophecy, as Menahim, who had prophesied to Herod that he should reign. "They serve God," said Philo, "with great piety, not by offering victims, but by sanctifying the spirit; avoiding towns, they devote themselves to the arts of peace; not a single slave is to be found among them; they are all free and work for one another." They were the only ones that taught man that he must and could be "Perfect, even as the Father in heaven is perfect;" and this was the constant teaching of Jesus to humanity. The rules of the Order were indeed strict; and, in order to enter upon training with them, it was necessary, as in the case of the boy Jesus, that the parents should be willing to give the Brotherhood absolute control over the child until it became of age, when the man could do as his conscience ordered him. In case one of age desired to enter, he had, after making application, to live a perfect and temperate life for one year before he was even admitted to training. After he was admitted he had to study under the brothers for another two years; and, if they found him worthy, he was then, at the end of three years after making application, admitted to the training for Mastership. Thus, in many cases, as in the case of Jesus, the training was a matter of twenty-one years; and it is from this that the three sevens has become a sacred number.

THE SON OF GOD

Only after starting on the training were the students allowed to participate in the common meals of the Order, which were celebrated with great solemnity and constituted one of the inner services of the Essenes, for each meal was a sacrament. The garment they wore was a white, flowing robe; and these, since they wore them only during these sacraments, were considered sacred. These fraternal love-feasts, the type after which Jesus instituted his "Lord's Supper," were begun and ended by prayer.

The Essenians taught the essential doctrines of both the Orphic and the Pythagorean Doctrines; the pre-existence of the soul, the consequence and reason of its immortality. According to Josephus, they claimed that "the soul descending from the most subtle ether, and attracted into the body by a certain natural charm (or vibration), remains there as in a prison; freed from the bonds of the body, as from a long servitude, it joyfully takes its flight." This same doctrine was understood and taught by Jesus when he asked: "Who say they that I, the Son of Man, am?" They, the disciples, of whom some were Essenians, replied: "Some say that thou art John the Baptist, some Elias, and others Jeremias, or one of the prophets."

"Among the Essenes, the brothers lived under a community of property, and in a condition of celibacy, cultivating the ground, and, at times, educating the children of strangers. The married Essenes (to whom Mary belonged) were a class affiliated with and in subjection to the other, (as is the Temple of Illuminati affiliated with the Rosicrucian Fraternity and under its direction). Silent, gentle, and grave, they were to be met with here and there, cultivating the arts of peace. Carpenters, weavers, vine-planters, or gardeners, never gunsmiths or merchants. Scattered in small groups about the whole of Palestine, and in Egypt, even as far as Mount Horeb, they offered one another the most complete hospitality. Thus we see Jesus and his disciples journeying from town to town, and from province to province, always certain of finding shelter and lodging. The Essenes were of an exemplary

THE SON OF GOD

morality, they forced themselves to transmute passion and anger (into benevolence, peace of mind and power to help others). Their word was more powerful than an oath, which, in ordinary life, they looked upon as superfluous, and almost as perjury. They endured the most cruel of tortures, with admirable steadfastness of soul and smiling countenance rather than violate the slightest religious' precept. (And of this we have an example in the crucifixion of Jesus.) From the Essenes Jesus received what they alone could give him: the esoteric tradition of the prophets, and by its means, his own historical and religious tendency or trend. He came to understand how wide a gulf separated the official Jewish doctrine from the ancient wisdom of the initiates, the veritable mother of all religions, though ever persecuted by the spirit of evil, of egotism, hatred, and denial, allied with absolute political power and priestly imposture (as indeed were all other ritualistic religions). He learned that Genesis, under the seal of its symbolism, concealed a theogony and cosmogony as far removed from their literal significance as is the profoundest truth of science from a child's fable. He contemplated the days of Aelohim, or the eternal creation by emanation of the elements and the formation of the worlds, the origin of the floating souls, and their return to God by progressive existence or generations of Adam. He was struck with the grandeur of the thought of Moses, whose intention had been to prepare the religious unity of the nations by establishing the worship of the One God, and incarnating this idea into a people."

"All these secrets which the patriarchs (masters) of the Essenes unfolded to the young Galilean on the solitary banks of the Dead Sea, in lonely Engaddi, seemed to him wonderful, but yet known, for in the past he had known the truths taught. It was with no ordinary emotion that he heard the chief (Master) of the Order comment on the words still to be read in the Book of Henoch (48 and 61): 'From the beginning the Son of Man was in the mystery. The Father kept him near his mighty presence, and manifested him to his elect... But the kings shall be afraid and shall prostrate themselves to the ground with terror, when they shall see the Son

THE SON OF GOD

of Woman seated on the throne of his glory... Then the elect shall summon all the forces of heaven, all the saints from on high and the power of God; and the Cherubim, the Seraphim, and the Ophanim, all the angels of Might, all the angels of the Lord, of the elect, and of the other Might, serving on earth and above the waters, shall raise their voices.' Jesus submitted to the discipline of the Essenes, studied with them the secrets of nature, and the occult power of healing. To develop his soul, he gained entire mastery over the body. Not a day passed without self-questioning and meditation on the destiny of humanity." (For this helped to awaken his conscience.)

It was a glorious day for him and for the others of the Brotherhood as well, when he received the highest teachings that the Order could give him, and when at last, instead of being the student, he became the master over that mightiest body of men then known to man. Henceforth he was free, master over his own actions, and recognized as the Supreme Hierophant of that Order which had taught him all the mysteries of both life and death. He had henceforth no master but his own conscience and the Christ within, which he had awakened, and which he had become, when he received Divine Illumination. Ever since his consciousness had sprung to life, he had found God within himself: for the fact that "Ye are the temples of the living God," had become manifest to him as had the certainty of the kingdom of heaven in the radiant beauty of his visions. Then came the suffering of humanity which had filled his heart with the awful outpour of its anguish. The wise Essenes had taught him the secret of religions and of the mysteries; they had shown him the spiritual decadence of humanity, and its expectation of a savior. But how could he find the strength needed to rescue it from the pit? And now, the direct call of John the Baptist fell on the silence of his meditations like a thunderbolt from Sinai- Am I to be the Messiah?

Jesus, now become the Christ, could answer the question only by the inmost meditation. Hence he retreated into the

THE SON OF GOD

wilderness on the forty days' fast as recorded in the Gospels. The temptation in reality represents in the life of Jesus this great crisis, this grand and sublime vision of truth, which all prophets, all religious Initiates, must invariably experience before beginning their work.

Thus did Jesus find himself in the cave of Engaddi, where all Initiates of the Order went for the final test. In his supreme suffering he cried unto the Most High God:

"By what sign, my Father, shall I overcome the powers of Earth?"

And the voice from within and from above answered:

"By the sign of the Son of Man."

"Show thou me this sign," cried the Son of Man.

Away in the horizon appeared a shining constellation, a rose, looking like stars in the sign of the cross; for there never can be a cross without the sign of life, and the sign of life is always the rose.

"The Nazarene recognized the sign of ancient Initiation, familiar to Egypt and preserved by the Essenes. When the world was young, the sons of Jophet had worshiped it as the sign of earthly and heavenly fire, the sign of life and all its joys, of love with all its wonders. Later, the Egyptian Initiates had seen in it the symbol of the Great Mystery, trinity dominated by unity, the image of the sacrifice of the Ineffable Being who breaks himself in order to manifest himself in the universe. Symbol at once of life, death, and the resurrection, it covered innumerable temples and tombs. The brilliant cross grew larger and came nearer, as though attracted by the heart of the Seer. The four brilliant stars (the rose) shone forth like suns of light and glory. 'Behold the magic sign of

THE SON OF GOD

life and immortality!' said the heavenly voice within. 'In ancient times it was in the possession of men, now it is lost. Willt thou restore it to them?'"

"'I will,' said the Christ."

"Strong in the gift of his very being, he now came to share with men this kingdom of heaven which he had won by meditation and by work, in torments of pain and boundless joy. He came to rend asunder the veil that had been cast over the ancient religion and that hid the new from view. He came to say: 'Believe, love, and act according to your belief and your love. Do deeds, rest not upon mere faith, for faith without works is dead. Beyond this earth there is a world of souls, a more perfect life. This I know, for I came from there; thither will I lead you. But mere aspiration for that world is not enough. To attain it, you must begin to realize it here and now, first in yourselves, afterwards in humanity.'"

He did not say that he was the Messiah, but discoursed in the synagogues concerning the laws and the prophets. He preached to the fishermen, by the fountains, in the oases of verdure abounding everywhere. He healed the sick by laying on of hands, or by a mere look or command, often by his presence alone; for it was by seeing suffering, diseased humanity, that the inner being was first aroused within him.

"Jesus went about in all Galilee teaching in their synagogues and preaching the gospel of the kingdom (of heaven), and healing all manner of sickness and all manner of disease among the people. And his fame went through- out all Syria; and they brought unto him all sick people that were taken with divers diseases and torments, and those which, were possessed with devils, and those which were lunatic, and those that had the palsy; and he healed them." Matt 4:23-24.

"The men of Capernaum knew him, and sent unto all that

THE SON OF GOD

region round about, and brought unto him all that were sick; and wherever he entered, into villages and into cities, or into country, they laid the sick before him in the market places and besought him that they might touch if it were but the border of his garment; and as many as touched him were made whole. There came unto him great multitudes, having with them the lame, blind, dumb, maimed, and many others, and they cast them down at his feet: he healed them insomuch that the multitudes wondered, when they saw the dumb speaking, the maimed whole, and the lame walking and the blind seeing; and they glorified the God of Israel."

"I and my Father are one."

This expression means the same as "God in me and I in you." By virtue of the union of men with the source of life and power, which comes to all men when they have found the Christ, as all must do if they will follow the instructions given by Jesus, man may heal the sick as he did; for did he not say:

"All things are possible to him that believeth."

There is no qualification to this statement; he said plainly that all things are possible to him that believeth. But this means that, if we believe in the laws that he taught, we will be willing to do as he did- we must think right, act right, and speak right. Besides this, like him, we must make deliberate efforts to reach the Christ Consciousness, or Soul Consciousness; for only through this consciousness can man acquire the power to do these things. In all respects, the Essenes taught exactly what Jesus taught during his ministry, and much of that which is now being taught by their successors, the Rosicrucian Fraternity and its branch, the Temple of the Illuminati.

THE SON OF GOD

THE SON OF GOD AND HIS CHRISTIC TEACHINGS

The teachings of Jesus deal largely with the "Son of man," and the "Son of God." According to the doctrine of Jesus, the "Son of man" is to become the "Son of God." The Son of man is the son of his earthly parents, endowed with the capability of becoming the Son of his heavenly Father. He was created by the Father in the beginning; and, though a son of man, he can, through the awakening of his mind, become the Son of God. In his teachings, Jesus deals with the aspirations of man toward the good. Good and worthy aspirations should be common to all men, and will help them in the realization of all worthy ambitions.

The Son of man can truly become the Son of God. This idea stands out clearly throughout the four gospels; but nowhere is it expressed more clearly than in the conversation with Nicodemus. (See "The Illuminated Faith; or The Christic Interpretation of St. Matthew.") Jesus taught that man, besides being conscious of a life born of the flesh of his father and mother, can also become conscious of a greater life- the life that becomes his through the Awakening.

"Verily, verily, I say unto thee, except a man be born of water and of the Spirit, he cannot enter into the kingdom of God. That which is born of the flesh is flesh; and that which is born of the Spirit is spirit. Marvel not that I said unto thee, Ye must be born again." St. John 3:5-7.

The body with its attendant personality, which we receive at birth into the world of sense, is the man of flesh. But that which a man receives after he has used the Awakened Mind to free himself from bondage to the senses and to the unholy desires of the flesh, is born in him of the Eternal One, whom we call God. This is the conscious self in man; it is the Soul; it is the "still, small voice" that speaks within; it is the knowledge, the realization, within the Center of Being, that man is Immortal. It is the consciousness of the Soul. Jesus said, in St. John 3:8:

"The wind bloweth where it listeth, and thou hearest the sound thereof, but canst not tell whence it cometh and whither it goeth; so is every one that is born of the Spirit."

This, which is born of God in us, this Son of God in man, must be exalted within us, that we may obtain the true life. He said:

"And as Moses lifted up the serpent in the wilderness, even so must the Son of man be lifted up."

The Son of man is the man of flesh, his nature is of the earth, so are his desires and his thoughts. Before he can know the Son of God and become like him, he must lift up the serpent; for the desires and the thoughts of the flesh are the serpent which Moses had to teach the children of Israel to lift up. He who lifts up this serpent, he who changes the thoughts and the desires from the earthly nature to the divine nature, will become the Son of God, and will know Him who is the Father. He who exalts, and prizes above everything else, the Son of God within himself, he who believes that eternal life is found in this divine element alone- he alone will be in perfect harmony with the laws of life; for the Conscious Being within is the light and the life of man, it is the Immortal Soul.

"Verily, I say unto you, except a man be born of water and of the Spirit, he cannot enter the Kingdom of God."

This is the doctrine of Regeneration. To be born of water is to have awakened to the fact that the earthly, or carnal, life is not the true, or the real, life. To become convinced of this fact we call the Awakening of the Mind; it is the Baptism with Water. He who has become awakened to this knowledge will then begin to use his

THE SON OF GOD

Awakened Mind in the building of a Soul. All his thoughts and desires will be changed. Instead of seeking carnal pleasures he will seek for that which is higher. He will use his mind for constructive thoughts; and this will bring about the re-birth of the Spirit, or Fire, which is the Illumination of his soul.

This is the development of the divine spark, or the divine spirit, in man. The spark of divinity is within all men, and only awaits the awakening, or the re-birth; then it is become the Christ. It was of this type of man that Jesus spoke when he said: "Ye are the temples of the living God," and again, "God in me and I in you." Without soul development, man cannot be "born again," nor can he be the temple of the living God; for God can dwell only in that which has become purified, that which is born of the divine nature.

According to the Christie Interpretation, water represents truth received intellectually. Unless we first receive truth with the mind, we cannot believe in it; but, unless we believe in something, we will not live and do accordingly. When the mind receives the truth, it is no longer a purely mortal mind; for it has awakened to a higher understanding, it is no longer bound by the carnal nature, but is open to the truths that belong to the divine nature.

Awakening to the truth will cause the mind to hold thoughts which have to do with the construction of the divine nature. These thoughts will purify the soul, and will begin the development of the divine spark; this means that man has begun the building of a Soul that shall be Immortal.

The new birth- which results in Consciousness of Soul or Baptism by Fire- signifies that the mind has assimilated the truth and that through the will man has used the truth as taught by the Divine Law in such a way that the truth has become his life. From this, results the victory of the soul over matter and the unholy desires of the carnal self; and the soul transforms the body into an

THE SON OF GOD

instrument that can be used for the accomplishment of the work given him to do on the earth plane. He who is now the awakened man becomes master of the body. As he attains mastery over the body, which is the instrument, he also becomes master over circumstances and conditions over which he formerly had no control whatever.

It is this mastery of the self that awakens the dormant faculties of man's being, opens the inner senses, and gives him intuitive insight into all truth, and a direct communion of soul with soul. Man then has become a Christ. This is the state of being, or of consciousness, of which Jesus spoke when he said:

"Ye are the temples of the living God."

Baptism by water is an intellectual baptism only, it is the awakening of the mind, it is the first step toward the accomplishment of the Great Work. Baptism by Fire, or the Holy Ghost, refers to the complete re-birth, the Conscious Illumination of Soul, or becoming the Christ or the Son of God. It is the awakening of the divine spark within man through the intelligence and the will; consequently, it leads ultimately to a complete regeneration of the whole being. Through this, comes to man the power to do all things, the power of the Christ. "I can do all things through the Christ which strengtheneth me."

Man is really a fourfold being: he is body, spirit, mind, and soul. The body is of the earth and must return to the earth when he is through with it. The spirit is the life of the body, and, coming from the Universal Storehouse, must return thither when he has finished using it. The divine spark is directly from God; and, if he does not awaken it and build it into a Conscious Illuminated Soul, it will also return to God, the Infinite Storehouse from which it came. The mind is a combination of body, spirit, and soul; or rather, it is the result of the combination of the three. If man obeys the voice of the body, which is the carnal earthly being, he builds

THE SON OF GOD

unto death; for in the flesh there can be no continued conscious existence. If he obeys the voice of the divine spark within, then does he build the great temple, the temple not made with hands, which is eternal.

'In speaking of the re-birth by water and by spirit, Jesus made allusion to a double transformation of the body. This regeneration must take place now, here on earth, before man passes through the stage called death. If he does not become "born again" of the water and of the fire while in the flesh, there is no opportunity for such re-birth until he returns again to the earth plane. "Ye must be born again," even as I, the Christ, the typical regenerate being, am said to have been born again, "of water and of the spirit." Though in person born of the Virgin Mary- which is, conceived in purity, and of the Holy Ghost- the Christ is none the less man's own soul and spirit restored to their original purity.

Born of the Virgin Mary, and hence conceived in purity, it was nevertheless necessary for Jesus, through acceptance of the teaching of John, and through the consequent baptism by water, or the Awakened Mind, to use this Awakened Mind in building the Soul and thereby in reaching Divine Illumination, which is the baptism of Fire, or the Holy Ghost.

Jesus taught man to exalt above all else the Son of man- not merely to exalt him through words of praise to an invisible God, but to exalt, to raise up, the Son of man, through constructive thoughts, pure desires, and worthy acts.

He taught to this effect: "When ye lift up, or honor, the Son of man, ye will know that I speak nothing from myself; for I speak not of myself but of the Father which sent me, He gave me a commandment that I should say and what I should speak." The Jews, not understanding these words, asked, "Who is the Son of man who is to be lifted up?" and Jesus answered them: "Yet a little While is the light in you. Walk while ye have the light, that

THE SON OF GOD

darkness overtake you not; and he that walketh in the darkness knoweth not whither he goeth."

Jesus did not bid them to worship him, but to follow the light which is in man and which he taught them how to find. "I speak nothing of myself" was his teaching. "Lift up the Son of man," he said to them; but he told them plainly that he was not speaking of himself but of them. All men are the Sons of man. In order that they may know the Christ, they must lift up themselves, they must change themselves from men of senses to men of Soul. Carnal desires must be changed, they must be lifted up, and become the desires of the Soul.

The light that is in man is the conscience. The voice of the conscience speaks to all men unless it is totally destroyed through continued evil acts, when the light is no longer with man. Therefore it is necessary for man to heed this voice, this light, and to follow it while it is still to be heard; for, if he does not do so, the time will come when the voice will no longer be with him.

To the question, "What does lifting up the Son of man mean?" Jesus answered, "To live in the light that is within man." No instruction could be plainer; for all men, unless the most degraded, know that there is something within man which accuses him when he does that which is not right. This is the light that is within man and it is this light which he must follow. As he obeys the voice, as he follows the light, so will it become stronger and stronger until it is a light that lights him through all things. All true religion consists in this one thing: To live according to the best one understands. No man can do wrong and say that the light within sanctioned it; for the light comes from the divine spark, and the divine spark sanctions no wrong. This light, if obeyed, develops into the Christ. As we follow the light we also follow the Christ; and with each good work, kind act, kind and loving thought, the Christ Child grows until at last he reaches manhood, and man has become the Son of Cod. From this light comes the conscience in

THE SON OF GOD

man. The voice is the conscience. Speaking further of the light in which men are to walk while they have the light within them, in Luke 2:35, Jesus says:

"Take heed therefore that the light which is in thee be not darkness;" and in Matt. 6:23, he says:

"If therefore the light that is in thee be darkness, how great is the darkness!"

The light can be darkened only through evil thoughts and evil deeds. If we follow the leading of the light, then does the light become brighter and brighter, and it leads to all good things. To follow the light means to hold pure thoughts, constructive thoughts, to do such deeds as will not only lead us upwards but will bring neither harm, loss, nor pain to a living being. Whereas, if the thoughts are evil and destructive, if our acts consider only the self for the time being and bring pain, loss, misery, and sorrow upon others, then are we continually darkening the light that is within us; and, if evil is persisted in, this ends in total darkness of the light. And how great is the darkness! For when once this darkness is complete, then has the divine spark been so completely covered with evil as to have lost the individuality it might have possessed in that human being; thus it only awaits the release that enables it to return to the Father whence it came and to enter once more on its mission in another life.

Before and since the time of Jesus on the earth, all true teachers have taught that there is within man a divine light, the light of reason; that it alone should be followed, be- cause in it alone can good be found. This was the teachings of the other Masters before Jesus, such as Brahmin, the Jewish prophets, Confucius, Socrates, Marcus Aurelius, and others. And when man follows this light and the divine laws as taught by the Masters, he is on the Path that will lead to Christhood.

THE SON OF GOD

The religious and the philosophical teachings of all times, all the systems with which mankind is acquainted, that of the Hebrews, of Confucius, of Buddha, Brahma, of the Grecian sages- all these are concerned with the regulation of man's life.

The entire intellectual activity of man should be centered in one thing- the working out of reason, of the ideas of good. Reason, which enlightens life and guides our conduct, is no illusion; it cannot be explained away. "Follow reason, illuminated by the divine light within, and attain welfare, not only of the self but of others," has always been the doctrine of all true teachers of mankind; it is the whole teaching of Jesus.

In giving the people the Divine Law, Jesus gradually taught them the truth as it was given to him. He maintained silence concerning himself unless he was asked directly. He told the people that the kingdom of heaven was at hand, that the Messiah would soon come. And now, after many centuries, how absurd to believe that he meant other than that the kingdom of heaven would come to those who should obey the Divine Law as he taught it; to those who, through development of the soul within, should find the kingdom within! For no one can find the kingdom of heaven unless he has first found the Christ through obedience to the Divine Law, and that means Soul Illumination, it means total Regeneration.

The kingdom of heaven did not come in a material sense; but it did come to all those who followed his instructions and who had found the Christ within themselves, as it will come to all those who now follow the same instructions.

In this connection, the saying of Jesus should be remembered: "Ye are the temples of the living God." And wherein can be the kingdom of heaven but where the Father dwells? If the body of man, when regenerated, is the temple of the living God, then must God dwell therein, and where God dwells there is

THE SON OF GOD

heaven. Matthew Arnold helped to make this mystery plain when he wrote:

> "Once read thy own breast aright,
> And thou hast done with fears;
> Man gets no other light,
> Search he a thousand years,
> Sink in thyself! There ask
> What ails thee- at that shrine."

Within man is to be found all that is, all that he may need, and all that he can desire. But before he can find this within, he must use the reason and the mind that he has, and build up the temple so that the light within him may shine and point the way to "the truth, the way, and the life."

Man seeks knowledge, happiness, health, success, peace, and love outside of himself. He expects to find it in the world of sense, only to be disappointed; and he seeks again and again, only to be disappointed again and again. These things cannot come from without. They must come from within; and when man once begins to use his thoughts aright, to direct his desires properly and to search within, then will he find all these things which he has so long been seeking from without in the senses of the flesh, where there is nothing to be found but the illusions of the flesh, and the fleeting moments of pleasure with the resultant hours of pain.

Browning sang:

> "Truth is within us all; it takes no rise
> From outward things, whate'er we may believe,
> There is an inmost center in us all
> Where truth abides in fullness; but around,
> Wall upon wall, the gross flesh hems it in."

In the Center of Being, which is the Soul, is all truth to be

THE SON OF GOD

found because it is a part of God, and therefore in direct communion with the fount of all knowledge. However, before we can go to this fount of knowledge, which is like a spring of water in the ground, we must break the gross flesh away, just as we would need to make a way to the spring in the ground.

This means that the flesh, which is the Son of man, must be lifted up. It means a process of change, a transmutation of the gross into the fine. This we can accomplish if we listen to the truth and obey the Divine Law. No man can find the fount unless he listens to this Law and obeys it; for, just as long as the unhallowed desires of the carnal man are gratified, just that long will the gross flesh continue to hem in the fount of truth.

In the Epilogue to "Honest Man," by Beaumont and Fletcher, we find:

> "Man is his own star; and the soul that can
> Render an honest and a perfect man
> Commands all light, all influence, all fate;
> Nothing to him fails early or too late."

In this, is the conviction that we are the masters of our fate; that the Soul, when once builded, is the star that leads us to all things; the Soul that has become illuminated, through the instrumentality of the body, will be able to master all things.

The body is the ship of which the soul is the captain; and there is not a sea over which this ship, with this captain, is not able to sail.

We are then truly masters of our fate. It rests with us what we will to be. It rests with us what we will, or will not, do. With us is the responsibility; for, if we will, we can accomplish all things. All those who have reached Soul Consciousness have taught the same great truths. They have been in different walks of life: one a

THE SON OF GOD

lonely carpenter; another a cobbler; another a laborer on the farm; and still another a poet. But each and every one of these has taught the one sublime truth, that within man is to be found all power if he will only overcome himself.

The apostles were always whispering to one another: "It is he!" and repeating the same to others. But Jesus, with gentle dignity, simply called himself "the Son of man." This title indicates that he was, as are all, the Son of man, but that he had found within himself the Christos, which is the Illuminated Soul, and that he was conscious of being the temple of the living God. He was conscious therefore of being a messenger to suffering humanity and of having a message, which, if obeyed, would lead them also to the Father and enable them to find the Christos within. To the claim that he was the Son of man, he added: "The foxes have holes and the birds of the air have nests; but the Son of man hath not where to lay his head." Influenced by the popular Jewish tradition concerning the Messiah, the simple hopes of the disciples conceived of the kingdom of heaven as being a political government, of which Jesus would be the crowned king and they the ministers. To combat this idea and radically to transform it, revealing to the apostles the true Messiah, the spiritual royalty; to communicate to them the sublime truth he called the Father, the supreme force he called the Spirit, mysteriously uniting all souls with the invisible; to show them and all mankind, by his work, life, and death, that he was a true Son of God; to leave them and all mankind the conviction that they were all his brothers and could join him if they wished; and, finally, to interpret to them, only after opening to their longing eyes the whole mystery of the Divine Illumination, an Illumination in which all men might share- this was the work that Jesus desired to do.

The Son of man and the Son of God are one. According to the doctrine of Jesus, the highest manifestation of God is he who, in constitution, form, intelligence, and work, is become the image of the universal Creator; he whose faculties, through obedience to

THE SON OF GOD

the Divine Law, have become like those of the Father.

Why is it that we, though Sons of God, know not our Father? Let the answer to this question be according to Isaiah 59:2-11: "Your iniquities have separated between you and your God, and your sins have hid his face from you, that he will not hear. For your hands are defiled with blood and your fingers with iniquity; your lips have spoken lies, your tongue hath muttered perverseness. None calleth for justice, nor any pleadeth for truth; they trust in vanity, and speak lies; they conceive mischief and bring forth iniquity... Their works are works of iniquity, and the act of violence is in their hands. Their feet run to evil, and they make haste to shed innocent blood; their thoughts are thoughts of iniquity; desolation and destruction are in their paths. The way of peace they know not; and there is no judgment in their goings; they have made themselves crooked paths; whosoever goeth therein shall not know peace. Therefore is judgment far from us, neither doth righteousness overtake us: we wait for light, but behold obscurity; for brightness, but we walk in darkness. We grope for the wall like the blind, yea, we grope as they that have no eyes; we stumble at noon day as in the twilight; among them that are lusty we are as dead men."

Here we have the reason why man does not know his God; why he does not know that he is a Son of God; and, consequently, why he is a poor human weakling, the victim of fate, the slave of every passion that is capable of giving pleasure even for a moment.

His hands are defiled with blood, not the blood of creatures which are in a less advanced stage of growth than he and which have not the divine spark within, but the blood of his fellow beings- beings who, very often, are farther advanced than he himself, and may even have attained Soul Consciousness.

He has on his hands the blood of beings who are equal

THE SON OF GOD

with himself and who, like him, are the Sons of man and who might become the Sons of God. He has on his hands the blood of the innocent; for he exploits the innocent in order to gain profit therefrom.

His lips speak lies in the hope of receiving benefit thereby; for through lies and through the subtlety of his tongue does he rob the neighbor whom he is commanded to love.

Through violent methods he obtains that which does not belong to him. Nothing is too brutal for him to attempt to do so long as it will bring him either pleasure or profit; and all this, not because he is striving for something eternal, but for that which gratifies for the passing moment only.

The man of flesh cares not for peace. No attempt does he make to gain the peace that all men should seek. He glories in war, in contention, in brutality, in exploitation of the innocent. All to him are but as prey; and he preys upon them as does the wild beast upon the quivering flesh. And yet, he is the son of man, with the possibilities of becoming the Son of God. However, he has not yet developed to that stage wherein he is truly man, and wherein he seeks for that which will give pleasure not only to himself but to others as well.

Not yet has he learned to know that there is pleasure only in that which gives benefit not only to the one but to the many; that there is profit only in that which profiteth the many as well as the one. When he comes to know this, he will seek for true profit, which robs no one, but gives to the many; for true pleasure gives pain to no one, but gladness to all that share in it. For, when his mind awakens to the truth, he will learn the right use of all things. His eyes will open to the truth; he will seek the ways of truth, knowing that in the ways of truth he will not be groping in darkness, but will be walking in the path of light.

THE SON OF GOD

The path of light leads to life. Only in the Illuminated Soul which is created by the Awakened Mind, is there true life, for this life is not for a day, but for eternity.

Two thousand years ago, John the Baptist said to men: "The time is fulfilled, and the kingdom of God is at hand, bethink yourselves, and believe in the Gospels," Mark 1:15, and "And if ye do not bethink yourselves ye will perish," Luke 13:5.

But men did not listen to these admonitions; and the destruction foretold has continued from that time on to this, and will continue until men learn to obey this command, which is a Divine Law.

The time is now, those that desire progress and regeneration must obey the Law. Not only is it necessary to have faith in the Law, but it is necessary to live in harmony with its requirements.

The millions are perishing, going toward destruction. All about us there is war, truly the blood of the innocent is upon the hands of men. For the sake of personal ambition, nation is warring against nation, and thousands are going down in the path of deterioration, having the blood of their fellow men on their hands.

Others are taking advantage of those who are still the slaves of circumstances. Some of these are caged up under ground; others, in the wilderness of woods; others, little children, in factories unfit for the lowest beast of the field. All those who exploit these helpless ones have the blood of the innocent upon their hands and therefore cannot know their God.

Unless man bethinks himself he shall perish. To bethink himself is to become awakened to the truth; for man does not bethink himself unless he first sees that the life he is living is irrational, unless he sees that the life of the senses is but a

THE SON OF GOD

temporal life.

When he awakens to the truth, when he bethinks himself, then will he consider the Divine Law as taught by Jesus. Then will he ask himself whether it is right, under any plea, to contemplate the murder of man; and as he bethinks himself he will remember the Law: "Thou shalt not kill." And as he continues to reflect he will know that whatever brings profit to one and works harm to another is under condemnation of the Law that says: "Thou shalt not steal." And he will be forced therefore to desist. As he awakens more and more, so will he bethink himself more and more; thus will he gradually come to understand the Divine Law and to work in harmony with it.

As he does this, so will his inner faculties awaken. He will begin to use them as the child begins to walk; and, gradually, as he continues to obey the Divine Law and gains strength and grows into Sonship, so will he find that there is a pleasure without pain, a profit without robbery, and a life without murder.

Each man is responsible to God for his acts. No man can plead that he has been forced to do wrong by some one else. To make this plea is but to admit that he is the slave of circumstances. And no man can be the slave of circumstances or of some one else, unless he is first of all a slave to himself, to the carnal self, to the man of flesh.

He who pleads guilty to slavery to the self, the carnal desires, pleads guilty to all else; for that man still lives the life of the flesh. And in the flesh there is not life, but death.

The first step to freedom is to become master of the self; to free the real man from the carnal desires. For it is these desires that lead a man to rob, to kill, to lie, to exploit the innocent, and to commit other wrongs, which in the nation leads to war, rapine, murder, and other crimes.

THE SON OF GOD

It is therefore necessary that salvation, or the new life, or regeneration shall come to the world through the individual. It is only as the individual learns the truth and obeys the Divine Law that the nation can be saved; for when the individual learns the Law, and obeys it, he refuses to live as he lived before. And through the example of the one will others come to do as he does.

No man can plead that he has been forced to war against his fellow man. The Divine Law recognizes no such thing as compulsion; and man is held responsible for what he does because he has been given free-will to do or not to do.

He cannot plead force, for he is given a mind with the faculty of reason. He must ask himself the question, Is it right to do this, is it right to do that; and if the answer indicates that it is not right, then he must refuse to do it. He must refuse to do it even though he may lose the life of the body; for "he who loses his life shall gain it."

He who has awakened to the truth, whose mind has become imbued with the Divine Law, will recognize nothing but his duty to man. He will obey the Laws of the Father, as does the workingman obey the directions of the one who is above him and gives the orders. He knows that the Father understands; and the voice within tells him that it is well, and he obeys. His is not a blind faith; for he walks not in darkness, but walks in the light. And the light teaches him all things; for the light comes from God, because it is the light of the Father.

For this reason, no man who knows the Father can uphold destruction of life, whether guilty or not. He knows that all life is sacred and that no life can be taken without incurring penalty upon the guilty one. For this reason, the man who has awakened, who has found the Path that leads to Divine Illumination, cannot uphold war. War is not made right simply by being sanctioned by organized society, which is called a government, but which in

THE SON OF GOD

itself is composed of individuals who are themselves personally responsible to God, and who, though combined, have no more right to sanction murder than has the individual man who stands alone. Might, under the Divine Law, does not make right. And it is just as evil, just as destructive to the soul, for many men in combination to commit wrong as it is for one man alone.

"Thou shalt not kill," has come down to us from the ages; for the Law holds that he who takes life shall lose his own life. No one can go contrary to the Divine Law without suffering its extreme penalty.

"Ye have heard that it was said by them of old time, Thou shalt not kill; and whosoever shall kill shall be in danger of judgment; but I say unto you, that whosoever is. angry with his brother without a cause shall be in danger of the judgment; and whosoever shall say to his brother, Raca, shall be in danger of the council; but whosoever shall say, Thou fool, shall be in danger of hell fire. Therefore if thou bring thy gift to the altar, and there rememberest that thy brother hath aught against thee, leave there thy gift before the altar, and go thy way; first be reconciled to thy brother and then come and offer thy gift. Agree with thine adversary quickly, whilst thou art in the way with him; lest the judge deliver thee to the officer, and thou be cast into prison. Verily, I say unto thee, Thou shalt by no means come out thence, till thou hast paid the uttermost farthing." Matt. 5:21-26.

Not only shall we not kill, but we shall not have anger against any one. To be angry is not only to hurt those against whom we hold anger, but it is a passion that creates a poison within our own organism. This poison we diffuse through the whole being, creating inharmony, sickness, failure, and often the beginning of conditions that tend toward disintegration. Anger is of the negative side of life, it is an evil. Therefore it is said to be "of the devil," because the devil personifies all that is destructive, all that leads not to life but to death. Holding anger against any

THE SON OF GOD

one in itself results in "the judgment," because it brings harm to ourselves. And it must be remembered that injury and harm to oneself is evil as truly as injury and harm to another.

This also has direct reference to those who, under the guise of religious authority, bless men that go to war, as truly as to those who themselves go into the field to take the life of their fellowmen. Those who actually enter war are often under some mistaken idea of right and justice, even led so to believe by men who would profit directly by such authorized murder.

If a man has aught against his brother, not only the brother of the flesh, but any one of the human family, his gift, which may be a prayer to the Father, cannot be accepted by Him until he has first made peace with the brother.

No man can hold two contrary emotions in his heart at the same time. It is impossible to hold the love of God in the heart and at the same time to entertain hatred or the desire to do evil to any man. So long as there is an inclination to bring harm to any of the human family, just that long will one's gift not be acceptable to God. Before prayer can be acceptable to Him who is All Love and who will not even punish those that hate Him, it must be freed from all desire to bring pain or suffering or misery to one of His creation.

But, says the seeker, what shall take the place of war in righting the wrongs committed by one nation against another? The answer to this is really easier than it might seem; for war, which is in itself one of the greatest evils, will never right another evil. Corrective methods should be made use of in righting all wrongs.

A corrective method can be found in the absolute shunning of the nation that is in the wrong until such time as she will make right the wrong. Practically all nations claim to be Christian- that is, to uphold the teachings of Jesus; but if they were truly Christian

THE SON OF GOD

they could not for a moment uphold wars. The only thing for Christian nations to do, when one of them does that which ordinarily would cause war, is completely and absolutely to cut all relations, business or otherwise, with that nation; for no nation, no matter how great, could bear being an outcast, having the mark of Cain upon itself, for any length of time.

You say this could not be done because it would interfere with business, work hardships, and lead to other difficulties. But really is this not done when there is war between nations? Besides this, is there not the vast expense of maintaining the war, and a vast amount of loss of useful lives? These two items- the shedding of blood and the robbing of people in order to maintain war- could be avoided, and the correction would be accomplished much sooner.

Take the murderer, for instance, set a mark upon him and free him so that mankind may know him to be a murderer. That man could not live among mankind for one month even though no man laid hands upon him. At first he might seem haughty; but every glance directed at him would have its effect. Though it might not really be true, he would think the glance was because of the mark upon him. Within a few days, his mind would be in such a state that it would be utterly impossible for him to look any other human being in the face; and this punishment of living among humanity while still being an outcast from humanity would become unbearable within a month. So with the nation that is in the wrong. At first it might attempt to face ostracism; but within a short time its condition would become unendurable and it would be very glad to make peace with the nation with which it is at odds and to repair the wrong of which it is guilty.

Corrective methods should be employed in dealing with nations as with the individual man. The men who bring about war are never the men who do the fighting, though this point seems to have been wholly overlooked throughout the past ages.

THE SON OF GOD

Lamennais wrote thus: "Towards the close of his mission Jesus proclaims a new society and fixes its foundations. Before him, nations were the possession of one or several masters, and belonged to these like so many herds. Everywhere the tyrannical domination of a few, and the servitude of the rest oppressed in the name of force or under the insolent pretext of superiority of nature. Princes and *grandes* cruised the world with all the weight of their pride and their rapacity. Then Jesus comes to put an end to this extreme disorder. He comes to lift the bowed-down heads; to emancipate these multitudes of slaves. He teaches them that, equal before God, men are free in regard to each other? that no one has any intrinsic power over his brother; that equality and liberty, these divine laws of the human race, are inviolable; that power henceforth can no longer be regarded as right; that it must depend on the association which delegates to it a function, a service, a devotion, a kind of slavery accepted by love in view of the welfare of all. Such is the society which Jesus commands his disciples to establish among themselves."

Is this the society that exists today? Is this doctrine which Jesus taught the one that rules the actions of men? Has this doctrine been made the law of life, of thoughts, of desires, of actions? Or has it been accepted purely as a matter of belief, a faith, one without works? To have these questions answered we need but look round about us. Everywhere there is strife. Everywhere wars and rumors of wars, everywhere the hand of one man against the other. And that which is worse, everywhere the hand of the strong against the weak, those not able to protect themselves, even against women and children, who should not be warred against but should be protected by the strong.

After eighteen hundred years, society is still in the same state as when Jesus taught the Divine Law to men. In many ways, it is even worse, for now has man advanced to a high state of development in so far as inventions are concerned. He is far better able to cope with the problems of life than in the foretime. But

THE SON OF GOD

with all this, he is even more the brute than he was before, for now he knows the truth, but refuses to accept it. Now he knows that the innocent should be protected; but he exploits innocence and even makes tariff of it.

He knows that womanhood is sacred; but, instead of paying homage to it, he curses it, debauches it, destroys it. In the foretime, men were taught that woman has no soul. But now man knows better, now he knows that she is equal with him, even greater than he; for she is not the coarse, brutal instrument of fate that he is. Yet, with all his knowledge, man has not become more humane, the self is not less ferocious, but is worse in many respects than it was before.

But the time is fast coming in which great changes will be made. The masses will no longer be ruled by the few unless they are ruled wisely. The masses, the people, are beginning to learn of the Divine Law; they are beginning to recognize the fact that to do that which is not in harmony with the Divine Law is to bring about its own punishment. Once they have fully learned this, they will no longer obey external masters in anything if they know that it is not for the good of all humankind.

The multitudes are beginning to seek for themselves. Up to this time, they have been willing to accept that which was given to them by those in authority, whether in matters of state, of law, of religion, or of economics. They are now beginning to awaken to the fact that there must be something wrong when the worthy are ground in the dust; when their sons are sent into the fields of war for that which does not in the least concern them; when their daughters are being sold by the thousands to the lowest forms of human life to be debauched, cursed, and cruelly destroyed; and when even their own wives are no longer protected.

They are awakening to all these things; and, with the awakening, is coming a search for the knowledge that leads to

THE SON OF GOD

freedom. Let a man learn that there is something radically wrong in a condition, and that it should not be so, and he is ready to begin the search to find out what it is that is wrong, and wherein is the fault. This search may extend over a longer or a shorter period; but, eventually, the search will end, and when he has found the remedy, you can trust him to use it.

There is one thing to be deplored: when men universally find the remedy, the tendency will be for all authority to be thrown aside and for anarchy to reign supreme until he finds that unrestricted action results in as great an evil as wrongly restricted action; but out of the turmoil will come obedience to Divine Authority and respect for wise leadership.

The work of the true teacher is to lead man to understand his weakness and his strength; to show him the action of the Divine Law; to point out to him wherein he must be under guidance and wherein he must be free. Once man is taught this, then will he have become truly man and not the plaything of circumstances.

"A wonderful and horrible thing is come to pass in the land; the prophets prophesy falsely, and the priests bear rule by their means; and my people love to have it so; and what will ye do in the end thereof?" Jeremiah 5:30, 31.

And this is true. Those who should teach the truth, the Divine Law, to the people are unwilling to do so because they fear that the people will forsake them. And why? Because if the Divine Law is taught to the people, they will thereby learn that to obey the Law makes men free; but they will also learn that individual responsibility is incurred by freedom. They must be taught that it is action which brings about results; that without a wrong action there can be no wrong result. No longer can they be taught that life is a matter of mere formal faith, that Immortality and eternal life can be had through mere verbal faith; but they must learn that the

THE SON OF GOD

only price for which Immortality of Soul can be bought is right thought, right desire, and right action.

Not an easy path is this to follow in the beginning, because it demands work in addition to faith. But once the work is begun, once man, through his acts, has begun to bring about right conditions, then will it be just as easy to follow righteous works as it was formerly to follow unrighteous works.

The priests of the people fear to teach the truth because there is danger that, if the people learn that faith in a creed can not save, they will forsake them (the priests). The priests suppose that only through hypocrisy can they hold the people to the church. This seems plausible, but is not true; for works begin in faith. He that teaches man a true faith first, and then shows him how to put his faith into practice, will be the one by whom an enlightened people will stand.

"Faith without works is dead." It is therefore necessary to have a faith that is founded on absolute truth, a faith founded on the Divine Law. To have a faith like this, results in work according thereto, and works in accord with a true, living faith will bring freedom from all bondage.

"He hath blinded their eyes, and hardened their hearts; lest they should see with their eyes, and perceive with their hearts, and should turn, and I should heal them." John 12:40.

It is the flesh with its carnal desires which blinds the eyes, the reason, of humankind. It is the flesh that desires this and that; and, as the unhallowed desires of the flesh are obeyed, the voice of the soul is hushed. The man in authority takes great care to keep humanity living in the desires of the flesh only; for well does he know that, when man is freed from the unworthy desires of the flesh, he is also freed from slavery to others who profit by that slavery. The first step in freedom is therefore for man to free

THE SON OF GOD

himself from his own carnal, or fleshly, desires. When he has accomplished this, he will become free from all other undesirable conditions, from all bondage, no matter what may be its nature. It is Satan, that which is of the flesh, which blinds the eyes of the people; and it is the fear of taking an unfamiliar step that holds humanity back from advancing in the light.

"Be not afraid of them which kill the body, but are not able to kill the soul; but rather fear him which is able to destroy both body and soul." Matt. 20:28.

And who is it that can kill the soul? None can kill the soul within us except ourselves. Other men can take the life of the body from us; but, if we allow them to take that life from us because we are enlisted in a righteous cause, we only gain thereby a greater life. Them we should not fear, no matter what they may attempt to do; but our own wrong thoughts, wrong desires, and wrong acts-these we should fear; for these end in destroying not only the body but the soul as well.

Even though men may command us to do things which we know to be evil, we are not forced to obey. The extreme penalty of man-made laws may be loss of the life of the body; but much is gained through this. But if we do the things that evil-minded and self-interested men command us to do, we not only lose the life of the body but we destroy the soul as well. Well does Matthew teach us not to fear him who might destroy the body, but to fear those things which are able to destroy both body and soul.

And among the greatest of these evils is that which men call war; for it is here where we commit all those crimes which are strictly forbidden by the Divine Law. It is through obedience to carnal-minded men, often men without souls, whereby we do those things which destroy both body and soul; for the Divine Law does not allow us to plead compulsion. There is no compulsion recognized by the Divine Law since all men are individually

THE SON OF GOD

responsible and have the privilege of either obeying or disobeying the commands of men.

Only God and the Divine Law are to be obeyed; and man only when he is working in harmony with the Divine Law and for the good of mankind generally. The refusal of man to obey an unjust order even though he might thereby lose his life, was borne in mind by Jesus when he said: "He that loseth his life shall find it." Matt. 10:31.

If all men, especially those who are called Christian and who claim to be followers of the lowly Nazarene, would refuse to bear arms against their fellowmen, war and bloodshed would soon be a thing of the past.

The truth is, men never have been taught to obey the teachings given by Jesus, which we call the Divine Law; but, instead, they have been taught to have faith in Jesus, as a personality, and thereby to expect to be saved. This has given man full liberty to do all manner of evil, and all this with the sanction of the priests who are supposed to be the leaders of the people in the place of Jesus. For this reason, evil has been the ministering angel these thousands of years, and will continue to be until man awakens to the fact that, not through belief in a personality, no matter how sublime, is life given to him, but through living a life identical with the life of the great Master Jesus. Not through faith alone do we reach Immortality, but through obedience to the Divine Law and through consequent Illumination which obedience to the Divine Law gives to man.

"Greater love hath no man than this, that a man lay down his life for his friends." John 15:13. And who is our friend? All men are to be classed as our friends. Each being belongs to the human family, and consequently each one should be a friend to the other. Hate cannot destroy relationship. Relationship is a thing that is, and always will be. And when we refuse to comply with man-

THE SON OF GOD

made mandates to go to war, then are we truly obeying the Divine Law; and if, through that act of refusal, our life is taken, then we have done the greatest thing that man can do- we have laid down our life that another may live.

But, says the seeker, if you do lay down your life in that way, another will simply take your place. Granted. But we have nothing whatever to do with the actions of another. Each man is an individual. Each man is individually responsible for that which he does. There can be no plea that he was forced to do thus and so. Nor can he set up the plea that others did so and so. He deals only with himself and his God, and is responsible only for himself and his acts. That which others do is not an example by which we can be saved. Our only guide is: "What says the Divine Law of my own Being?" Only in obedience to the Divine Law is there safety, only there will we find a guide to life, a guide to death, a guide to Immortality.

"Thou shalt not kill" is a law that stands out in letters of fire; and no nation can be truly Christian so long as it upholds war. Nor is it possible for any man to be Christian while believing that wars are desirable ; for to be Christian is not only to be a believer in the doctrine as taught by Jesus, but to be one who does as Jesus did. "For all they that take up the sword shall perish with the sword." Matt. 26:52.

Here again we have the Divine Law, which is absolute and which clearly states that as we do to others we shall be done by. There is no qualification in this statement whereby one is released from the penalty. Considering the fact that for thousands of years nation has been against nation and man against man, can there by any wonder that the earth is one great field of groaning souls- souls which are wringing in misery, in sorrow, in trouble, in disease, and in failure?

And what is the base and the cause of all this misery?

THE SON OF GOD

Simply the unholy desires of the self; for each one that suffers has brought the suffering upon himself through disobedience to the Divine Law.

Not only has this great principle reference to the one evil of taking the life of another, but it has equal reference to all actions of life. Just as he who takes life stands in danger of losing his life in the same manner, so he who cheats stands in danger of being cheated by one on the same plane of being as himself. He who steals stands in danger of being stolen from by some one of no greater development than he; and he who takes advantage of the weak stands in danger of receiving a similar injustice or of seeing one of his own loved ones suffer injustice at the hands of another.

The Law is absolute, and no one can escape it, and no one can be free from these evils until he first frees himself from them. All of them are due to one's own personal bondage to the unsanctified desires of the carnal self.

It is not wrong to gratify desires for those things which bring no harm or sorrow either to the self or to others. Man is not forbidden pleasure that brings harm to none; for he is not supposed to live in self-denial except in respect to things which can harm either the self or some one else.

And in this do we find the standard for life. The standard to place before oneself should be: I desire this thing, it will give me satisfaction, it will give me joy; but in the gratification will it hurt myself or will it hurt another or bring sorrow to another? If the answer is that no harm is liable to result from it, then are we free to enjoy it.

"Therefore all things whatsoever ye would that men should do to you, do ye even so to them." Matt. 7:12.

THE SON OF GOD

In this, we have the law and the prophets, for it is a complete code for action. Were men to obey this standard, there would be no hate, for no man desires to be hated. There would be no robbery, for no man desires to be robbed. There would be no murder, for no man desires to be murdered. There would be no exploitation, for no man desires to be exploited. There would be no profit made out of the innocent, for no man desires that those who are innocent and who are near to him shall be betrayed. Battlefields would be sown with the grains that give food to the millions. Swords would be turned into plowshares. Jails would be turned into schools where the laws of life would be taught. Navy yards would become manufacturing places, while those who are at the head of the navy would be superintendents over men who perform useful labor, labor which would be to the profit of mankind universally.

Were this law obeyed, then men would seek to do the right; and seeking the right, they would be seeking the Christ, and soon would all men in truth be the Sons of God. As all men are equal before the Creator, all men should truly seek for the good of each other. In doing this, they would establish the universal brotherhood, and Christ would be ever among them. Religion, as now understood, would not be; for all men would live as ordained by God, and consequently religion would be their habitual manner of life and their habitual type of thought. But the law that man has not yet been able to understand, is the fact that he must be subject to the principle of love and good-will to others.

For this very reason, if man hates another even secretly, through the action of the Divine Law, or through the law that we call attraction, he will receive hatred from another. Under the same law, if a man cheats another, he will be cheated or suffer some loss in return for that which he did. Again, he that causes suffering to another will be made to suffer in some way. Indeed, his suffering will be greater; for he not only pays the debt he owes, but he also pays interest on the debt.

THE SON OF GOD

This Law is absolute and covers every action of man. Whether he does good or ill, he will be sure to receive good or ill as the case may be. This is covered by the law that says: "He that taketh life by the sword shall perish with the sword."

This being true, would it not be better for man to obey the Law in the first instance, and thus avoid the penalty? His advancement would be faster, his achievements and his pleasures greater, and there would be no old debts to pay. But men have been led to believe that the chief aim of life is to gain honor, fame, money, or the many other things usually thought of as bringing happiness. It is a mistake to consider this the chief aim of life. Man's highest duty is service to those less advanced than he; and, through service, will he achieve greater enlightenment, have greater pleasures, and obtain more power, although it may require a longer time, than if he labors only for the self.

This one principle, "Do unto others as ye would that they should do unto you," is the greatest of all. It includes all the commandments, and is the basis of true, undefiled religion. There is nothing greater than this.

Sixteen hundred years before the birth of Jesus, there was an Egyptian saying: "He sought for others the good he desired for himself. Let him pass on."

This is a wise saying, and all men should heed it. If man would try to help others to obtain the things that he desires for himself, he would himself obtain them; for we can do nothing for others, no matter what it may be, without sharing its benefits. Whether our deeds be good or ill, the principle is absolute that whatever we give to another we will receive for ourselves.

Thirty-four hundred years prior to the present time, when the Hindu kingdom was being established on the Ganges, it was written: "The true rule of business for men is to guard, and to do

THE SON OF GOD

by, the things of others as they do by their own."

What a contrast between such a system of business and the present one. Then the interests of others were watched. Now, each man cares only for his own interests, and his affairs will he push forward, no matter how many millions are the victims in his path. Man cares not if he crushes out the life of unborn babes, if he sacrifices the virtue of the innocent, if he crushes the men who have the interest of their families at heart. His business, his profits, must be watched and carefully nurtured at the expense of all else. And what is there at the end of life for such? Darkness and death. Nothing can go with them, the profits remain for those to enjoy who had nothing to do with the accumulation. The body returns to mother earth; and the soul, less an individual than when it left the Father, returns to Him.

Twenty-five hundred years ago, Lao Tze wrote: "Requite injury with kindness." "To the not good I would be good in order to make them good."

Our penal code has forgotten all the divine laws, if indeed it ever knew them. The Law of Hermes was "As it is above, so is it below." According to this principle, the laws of the country and the state should be in harmony with the Divine Law, and therefore all methods of punishment should be corrective. But such today is not the case, the laws of the state and of the country are directly opposed to the Divine Law; and the methods are not corrective but destructive. This does not mean that those who manifest criminal tendencies should be turned loose on society at large, but that jails and penitentiaries should be institutions of learning-places where men are taught the principles of right and justice, where they are taught some useful labor, and where they are shown that the wages of sin is death.

No criminal has ever been reformed through the brutality of modern methods of correction or punishment. The criminal is

THE SON OF GOD

already bitter against organized society; and well he may be, for it is generally admitted that the methods of organized society are defective. To punish is not to arouse the better nature of him who is punished, and to make it sweeter.

Man is an animal only so long as he is ruled by the animal senses; but, when man once understands that it for his own best interests to change these animal tendencies, then is there hope of his reformation. This never comes about through the medium of fear; for fear holds men in check only so long as they think there is something to fear. It must come through a system of training, the basis of which is love. Men can be appealed to through the better side of their nature, and taught that it pays them, individually and collectively, to hold the better side uppermost. You cannot make men good by being cruel to them, by showing hate in every glance, by giving them less to eat and to wear than they need, and by caging them like some wild beast. You can make them good by being good to them, by showing them that there is that within them which is God-like but which they are now degrading. The professional reformer cannot do this, for he attempts to do one thing while leading a life that is contrary to his actions. Such men manifest through the personality just what they are, and no one feels this quicker than the criminal.

The Greeks in 1070 B.C. came yet nearer to the wording of Jesus: "Do not that to thy neighbor which thou would take ill from him."

The law under which men live at the present time has nothing whatever to do with consideration for the other man, but only with consideration for the self. The question is not: What can I do for you? but What can I get out of you? The Divine Law, and the Law under which all men must come sooner or later, is simple as to what is best for all. Understanding of the Law simply means knowing that exactly as we do to another, so will we be done by. This is true, not because God rewards or punishes, but because

THE SON OF GOD

with every act we set into motion a law that affects us as directly as it does the one with whom we deal.

This does not advocate that the laws under which men now live should be set at naught at once and without notice. That would mean anarchy and chaos. But men should be taught the Divine Law, and gradually they should replace the present laws that are contrary to the divine laws with requirements and standards that are in harmony with the Divine Law. Only in this is there protection, and all things must proceed in an orderly manner.

The Hebraic law taught this same truth. In a parchment, believed to have been the first inscribed some twenty-five hundred years ago, is to be found: "Whatsoever you do not wish your neighbor to do to you, do not that to him." Appended to it was this statement: "This is the whole law. The rest is mere exposition of it." If this is a reliable index to their standards, it seems that the Hebrews of that far-off time were far wiser than are we of the present civilization; for they then recognized and taught that which mankind generally has ignored, namely; that all reform, no matter what its nature, begins with the individual. As the individuals so is the village; as the villages, so the county; as the county, so the state; and as the states, so the nation.

If men would uphold this one rule, not merely according to the letter, but in actual practice, then they could do no wrong, either to themselves or to another; and, being right themselves, they would not allow any law to be made that is out of harmony with the Divine Law.

Confucius advised: "What you would not wish done to yourself, do not unto others." And this is but a re-statement of that taught by all the others. It is therefore true, that those who had received Illumination of Soul through obedience to the Law in thoughts, desires, and acts, state the same principle, no matter how distant in space or in time they lived one from the other. In the earliest known written manuscript of Ptah Hotep in Egypt five thousand five hundred years ago, thirty-five hundred and fifty years before the time of Jesus, is found this inscription: "If thou be among people, make for thyself love the beginning and end of the heart."

Just as he who lives by the sword shall die by the sword, so he who lives in love will die in love. The house that is erected upon a firm foundation shall stand firm against all storms, and that which is built upon the sand shall pass away with the first tempest. So the life in harmony with the Divine Law is sure to exist unto all eternity; for love is at once the beginning and the aim of life. In love, or through love, are all things possible, It is the path that leads from the beginning of the earth-life, or the experience- life, to Immortal Illumination, which is the eternal life.

The Christian standard reads thus: "Thou shalt love thy neighbor as thyself." It may seem that the word, neighbor, limits one's duty. But, in its broader sense, it means the same thing as that which Ptah Hotep taught; for, if one can hold love in the heart for the neighbor, he is able to have love for all mankind. Love is not limited as to person nor as to locality, nor as to race or creed. It is that which is in the heart, and it is universal.

That love which is only for the neighbor at one's side is a selfish love because, as a rule, we love him only because he has been of some help, of some benefit, or profit to us; and such is not love of the neighbor, but love of the self- it is self-interest.

At the first Buddhistic Council held at Rajagriha in 466 B.C., the scribes almost duplicated the advice of Egypt's priest, in the writing: "One should seek for others the happiness one desires for oneself."

This is sound advice for this reason: Under the Divine Law we receive according to what we give another or help another

THE SON OF GOD

to get; only that, through the reactionary principle, we receive twofold. Consequently, when we seek to bring happiness to others, we set vibrations into motion which bring to us the very thing that we seek for others. The mere fact that others will not accept that which we desire to give them does not make void the Law. It is what we ourselves do that counts, and not what others do or what they accept.

A century and a half before the time of Jesus, the law of Rome once more repeats the theme: "The law imprinted on the hearts of all men is to love the members of society as themselves." Now, one may smile at Roman law, knowing how those at the head of society then used the people; but the action of men in no wise offsets the truth stated. Because men do not obey a law does not nullify the law. The Law is, whether men obey it or not; and it works just as surely when men do not obey as when they obey. If they obey, theirs is the reward of the Law; if they disobey, theirs is the punishment of the Law. The Law simply is. Jesus himself declared the Golden Rule, so called because it is at once the head and the foundation of all Laws.

When Alexander of Macedon marched into Persia, 334 B.C., he found there: "Do as you would be done by," which had been taught by Zoroaster. Since all countries and all ages have had such sublime statements of the Divine Law, why do we find men who exist by robbing their fellowmen, by cheating, by sending others to war, by trading in the innocent? The answer is simplicity itself: men do these things because they believe it to be to their interest to do so. One thing, which more than anything else explains men's actions, is that they regard these standards as religious, as belonging to the church and those that have to do with the church. No longer caring for religion, they think that these principles do not apply to them. They must understand that divine laws are not limited to religion; that religion is not their author; that they are practical conditions- conditions which are absolute in business and in all affairs of life because they are part of the

THE SON OF GOD

Divine Order of the universe. They must be led to understand that to violate any law of order and well-being- whether on the business, social, or economic plane- is to violate the Divine Law in that particular respect.

Man must learn that these laws are more than religious as usually understood, that they are not mere church laws; that they belong to no creed, no sect, no doctrine; but that they are universal principles, which should control all things in life, and which will bring true happiness, true success, and all other desirable things to those that obey them. The law of gravitation is not thought of as a religious law or code. The ethical law is as truly a law of the universe as is the law of gravitation. The principles of action are ethical or religious merely because they pertain to man in his relation to man. In their method and in their impartiality of operation, they function with as much precision as do the laws of magnetism and gravitation or any other law on the physical plane.

Religion should not be a creed, a dogma, something merely to believe in, it should be a mode of everyday life. Such a religion is, simply because it is life. People should understand that God is not afar off, a judge of our acts, one who either condemns or rewards us, but that He is the Good that is in man, in each one. Jesus truly taught: "Ye are the temples of the living God." If people understood these things, conditions would be far different from what they are.

And this good, this God in the temple of man, will become more and more known to man as he lives in harmony with the truth until finally he has become the Son of God, one with the Father; one with the power of God; one with Him as a sharer of all good things, including health, happiness, and success. Tolstoi, that master of the teachings of teachings, wrote:

"The law of human life is of such a nature that the improvement of life, of the individual as well as of society, is

THE SON OF GOD

possible only by inward moral perfecting. Whereas all the efforts of men to improve their life by external influence and coercion serve as the most effective propaganda and example of evil, and therefore fail not only to improve life but, on the contrary, increase the evil, which, like a snow-ball, continually grows larger and larger, and more and more powerful, and removes people from the only possibility of truly improving their life. All things, therefore, whatsoever ye would that man should do to you, do ye even so unto them; for this is the law and the prophets. When an evil occurs, as in the case when war is declared, all men are ready to take sides and when their loved ones are slain or worse, and the war is over, then they start to blame every one but the right one, namely, themselves. Men do not see that as they, singly, and collectively, uphold any form of law, they are each individually guilty of that very crime, provided it ends in crime as war always does. Men are prone to act for the worse and then blame others for it, when, had they followed the Golden Rule such a thing could not have occurred. It is thus with all people, even with the laborers. They are exhausted, crushed, enslaved, only because, for some miserable advantage, they themselves ruin their own lives and the lives of their brothers. Were each and every one to uphold the Golden rule, the working man would soon be one of the most independent and favored of the gods, of all men. Two thousand years ago a law of God became known to men, the law of reciprocity, that one should act unto others as one wishes to act to oneself. This law is so simple, comprehensible to every one, and obviously gives the greatest welfare possible to man. And therefore it would seem that as soon as men had learned this law they ought immediately, as far as possible, to fulfill it themselves, and to use all their powers to teach this law and its fulfillment to the rising generations. Especially would it seem that the men of our Christian world ought to act thus, recognizing as they do, as the chief divine revelation, that gospel in which it is explicitly taught that in this law 'is all the law and the prophets;' that is, all the teachings that are necessary for man, or for the salvation of man."

THE SON OF GOD

"And yet, almost two thousand years have elapsed and men not only refrain from fulfilling this law and from teaching it to their children, but in most cases they do not themselves even know it, or, if they do, they regard it either as unnecessary or as impractical; and yet, unless this one great law is fulfilled, a universal religion or universal peace cannot result. The law of God is the law of God not because, as priests would affirm about their laws, it has been communicated in a miraculous way by God himself, but because it unmistakably and obviously directs men to that way of advancing along the lines which unquestionably are delivering them from their sufferings, and unquestionably obtain the greatest inner and external welfare- not some few particularly chosen men, but all men without exception. Such is the law of God about acting towards others as one wishes that others should act towards oneself. It shows that men fulfilling it unquestionably obtain inner spiritual welfare, in the consciousness of their harmony with the will of God, and of the increase of love in themselves and in others; and that at the same time they obtain in social life the greatest possible welfare accessible to them. Whereas, divergence from the law entails aggravation of their position."

"The law of God is the law of God for this reason, that it defines the position of man in the world, showing him the 'best' that he can do for his spiritual as well as for his physical life in this position. 'Be not anxious,' said Jesus, 'saying, What shall we eat or what shall we drink, or wherewithal shall we be clothed?... Your heavenly father knoweth that ye have need of all these things. But seek ye first his kingdom and his righteousness (inner consciousness as being one with God) and all these things shall be added unto you.' If man fulfills what God requires of him, if he observes His law, then God also will do for him that which he requires. So that the law of doing to others as one would wish to be done to oneself relates to God also. For once man gets into harmony with the Father within, there is a certain power given to him by which, or through which, he obtains the things that he

THE SON OF GOD

needs. The principle of true religion is clearly expressed in the Gospel by the words: 'Do unto others as thou wouldst wish that others should do unto thee.' This is the whole law and the prophets. If this principle were recognized as the chief religious principle by all men, then egotism, which is the readiness to sacrifice one's neighbor's welfare to attain one's own ends, would disappear of itself. So that I recognize as the cause of evil in general, and of wars in particular, solely the ignorance of true religion. The only solution of the social problem for rational beings gifted with the capacity to love consists in the abolition of force, and in the organization of a society founded on mutual respect and rational principles voluntarily accepted by all. Such a condition can be obtained only by the development of true religion. By this term, I refer to the fundamental principles of all religions, which are: first, the consciousness of the divine essence of the human soul; and, secondly, regard for its manifestation."

"Ye are the sons of God."

That man is created in the image of the Supreme God, that he can be like God in all things, in goodness, in creative power, and all things else- this is the foundation of the Temple of Illumination and is the foundation upon which its whole Philosophy and all its principles are founded. In order to become the Son of God, one must do that which one's conscience, the inner self, indicates. One must say nothing except that which one knows to be the truth. If, for some reason, one is placed in a position in which one cannot speak the truth, it is best to say nothing, to remain silent. One must do what one sees as duty and not shrink from it, no matter how unpleasant it may seem.

Man cannot make the plea that he is forced to do this or that, in face of the fact that he has been given free-will by his Maker. If he is not the master of his will, of himself, of his personality, let him consider whether any one is to blame for it except himself. It is not possible for a man to come under the

THE SON OF GOD

compelling power of others unless he has first of all become a slave to the carnal desires of his own fleshly nature. If he is such a slave, it is not a hard matter for other men to force him to do things which he does not want to do; for he is no longer master of himself, but is in bondage to the lower self.

Nor must we think of the self in the work of self-mastery. We must think of that which is for the good of all; and, being for the good of all, consequently it will be for our own good. No man is sufficient unto himself.

First of all, we must live and think so that we may gain control, or mastery, over the lower, or the carnal, self. And, in accomplishing this, we must carefully consider the reason for our efforts- whether it is for purely selfish motives or because we desire to be that which God has intended us to be and because we desire others to become what their Maker desires them to become.

We must distinguish between the Self and selfishness. Selfishness applies to that which we do for ourselves alone, that which we work for, that which we wish to gain, not for the good of anyone else, but only for our own good, and even at the expense of others. That which is of the Self has to do with the inner being, the true man. If it is truly for the Self, we will do nothing that might bring the least harm or sorrow or loss to another in any way; but, rather, we will bring help to all others to whom it is possible to give help. In this way, do we truly help the Self- by, or through, helping others.

In this work of self-mastery, or seeking Soul Consciousness and Illumination of the being, it is possible that we are not as are the majority; but this does not matter. The one question is, whether we are in the right, whether we are working in harmony with the divine laws. If we are doing this, then we and God are a majority; for, if God is with us, none can be against us. Man must remember that God, the Father, the Creator of all things,

THE SON OF GOD

does not desire the spoken praise of men. He does not desire lip service, the service that comes only from the mouth. God desires to be praised, not by words, but by acts. He desires men to do the things that He is doing; and thereby they offer the greatest praise to Him that it is possible for man to offer.

Spoken praise counts for naught. Nor is faith without works of any value. It is in the thoughts, the desires, and the acts that we truly praise God; and this is the only praise that God, or the Divine Law, either accepts or recognizes.

We must first of all come to understand the Divine Law. When we understand this, then do we understand God, because the Law is God. In proportion as we understand the Law, it is our duty to obey the Law; and in obedience to the Law do we truly worship God, for then we do the works that the Father does also.

In nature all things obey the Divine Law. The tree is true to its nature and brings forth fruit only of its kind. The rose brings forth only a rose, emblem of all that is beautiful and true. The earth yields according to that which is sown; but man, having free-will, alone proves false to the trust placed in him.

But there is still a worse feature: man is ignorant of the fact that when he violates the Divine Law he hurts none more than himself. He does not realize that obedience to the Law will bring all the good things that he requires without the pain and the sorrow that disobedience causes. In laboring only for the self, in doing only those things which seem to profit himself, and which bring profit for the time being, he believes that he is preparing for the future, that he is storing up benefits for a time to come. Whereas, in reality, he is storing up conditions that will result in losses and sorrow. This fact man does not realize. If he is to become truly man, this is the truth that he must be taught. He must learn that only as he truly makes himself a part of the whole, laboring for the interests of the whole, can he become truly the partaker of good

THE SON OF GOD

things and therefore truly an individual. Only in individuality- devotion to the whole- is to be found Godhood, or Sonship with the Father.

This is true religion: not something to believe in, not some creed, nor some faith, out a method of living- a method that brings results not only on the plane of Soul Development out on the material plane as well. For, if we live right on the soulual plane, we will obtain results on the material plane also. Man cannot be right in regard to the interests of his soul and be a failure on the material plane. Therefore, true religion is something that is practical, that brings tangible results- results that are of benefit here and now, not reserved for some far-off time and place.

"Religion is the relation of man to the eternal life, to God, in accordance with reason and knowledge, which moves man forward towards the end for which he was intended."

This moving forward brings man into touch with all power. This power he can use in obtaining those things which will give him contentment, peace of mind and Soul, and all that he truly needs. It will bring health, for in health he finds joy. It will bring material success; for material success is the birthright of all men. The Father denies to the son nothing of which the son is worthy and in need. It is only those who are unworthy to whom these things are denied. Though it may seem that men who obey not the Divine Law are possessed of many things, it yet remains a fact that they are denied, through some cause or another, the pleasures that such possession should bring, and does bring, when possession is in accordance with the Divine Law.

The Soul of man is the Light of man; but, before he can make use of the light, he must first develop Soul Consciousness. The soul cannot give forth light until it has attained Consciousness; for only in Consciousness is there Illumination. In general, man is weak, he is inclined to be ruled by the flesh;

THE SON OF GOD

consequently, he is miserable, because, though having the potentiality of a god, he still is little more than an animal, and the animal nature and the divine nature are not as yet in harmony. He will continue to be an animal until such time as he seeks to know himself, until he masters the animal tendencies, and kindles the vestal lights on the Altar. This he cannot do until he first learns the Divine Law and obeys it. On the animal plane, he obeys the law of his animal nature. On the higher plane, he must understand and obey the Law of his Divine Being.

When he kindles the fires on the Altar at the center of his Being, when he brings the soul to Consciousness, to Illumination, then does he become the most powerful being on earth. He becomes the Son of God, the Christos; and in lesser degree he has the power of a God, the creative energy of the Father who is the creator of all things. It is of this God-man that Jesus spoke when he said: "These things, and even greater things shall ye do." The man who has found the Christ possesses the power of the Christ, and can use this power for the good of himself and for the good of mankind in general. In this way, does man become a conscious being, by realizing that he who was once but the son of man is the Son of God, and that he is the temple of the living God in proportion as he makes that temple a fit dwelling place for the Father, by lighting the lights upon the altar and by keeping them burning. Thus will the Father do His works through man.

The Christie religion is nothing less than the consciousness of man's relation to God- the highest consciousness of which humanity is capable. The Christic religion is not a creed, it is a consciousness, it is a state of being. It is not something merely to be studied, but something to be experienced, something into which we grow through a method of thinking, desiring, and living. It is something we find within us, something which belongs to the Divine Spark and which becomes the Illuminated, Conscious, Individualized Soul, as we think, desire, and act aright, or in accordance with the Divine Law.

THE SON OF GOD

Being the son of man, we must gradually ascend from the lowest, or the carnal, earthly, fleshly plane, to the highest step of the ladder, which is Soul Consciousness attained through the innate love of the heart for all that is good, for all that is pure, and for the good of the children of man.

The Christie religion, the method of living advocated by the Temple of Illumination, enables man to attain the highest degree of power, of knowledge, and of consciousness, because it teaches him the Divine Law, it shows him how to make the beginning and how to go forward, step by step, until the highest stage of development has been reached.

It is practical, in that it does not theorize, and in that it understands, and is able to teach, the Law. Moreover, it is practical because it takes into account the fourfold nature of man: the physical, or the material; the mental, or the intellectual; the spiritual, or the life-principle; and the soul, which is of God, and may become Individualized God Consciousness. It is practical because the laws that it teaches bring health to the physical being, knowledge to the intellect, fuller life and greater power to the spiritual nature, and absolute Illumination and sublime Consciousness to the Soul.

The Temple of Illumination with its Christie principles condemns nothing. It teaches the truth, it teaches man how to live according to the truth. Without favor, it condemns those acts of men and those conditions in life which are contrary to the Divine Law; but it condemns nothing that can lead to more abundant life, to greater unfoldment, and consequently to better manhood and womanhood. All men are brothers, because they are the sons of men and are born under the same universal laws. All men are brothers, in that they are parts of one great chain. Each one is a link, either weak or strong, as the case may be. Each one either remains as part of the chain or becomes detached from the chain through his own unworthy acts.

THE SON OF GOD

The true man is he who believes that God is the Father of all men and that man's highest welfare is obtained by recognizing his Sonship with the Father through obedience to the Divine Law, which is of the Father. And it must be clearly understood that man cannot come to recognize Sonship with God unless he thinks and desires and acts in harmony with the Divine Law; for, only through such thinking, desiring, and acting, can he grow into this knowledge, or this recognition.

Mere belief in the Fatherhood of God will never of itself bring Sonship; but, when one lives according to the belief, and thinks and acts according to it continually for any length of time, then does one grow into the knowledge, and, through the knowledge, is born the recognition.

The most pronounced distinction between true faith and its consequent works, and a corrupt faith is seen in this: when faith is corrupted, when it is a mere belief or creed, man expects God, in return for his sacrifices and prayers, to fulfill his own wishes; his prayers are little short of dictations to his Maker; he seems to expect the Creator to become his servant and to do according to his own requests. Whereas, true faith teaches man that God demands him to do the works of a man; that He expects man to do the works of a God; that He requires man to be the fulfillment of His Will; that He expects man to answer his own prayers through an intelligent application of the divine laws of life, and through the power of the Divine in and through him, God asks man to realize that he can do all needful things through the Christ within that strengtheneth him.

To become an individualization of the divine nature, or the Son of God, we must be like God. This means that we must be doers, not mere believers; that we must think, and act, and desire as God does. This means that we should be willing to help and to forgive our fellowmen; that we should feel called upon to do so. As for ourselves, we are absolutely responsible for all that we

THE SON OF GOD

think, all that we desire, and all that we do. We cannot plead that we have been harmed by another, cursed by another, or have suffered loss through another. Though God is cursed by man, he does not curse man in return, but forgives his acts. In reality, under the Divine Law, man curses himself rather than anyone else; and through his acts he brings about his own punishment.

"Then came Peter and said unto him, Lord, how often shall my brother sin against me, and I forgive him? Until seven times? Jesus said unto him, I say not unto thee, Until seven times: but, Until seventy times seven." Matt. 18:21.

In order to understand this better, it must be remembered that, if our brother offends us or sins against us, it is but seemingly so, because nothing except that which we think, desire, or do ourselves can truly injure us. Only for our own acts are we responsible, and only for our own acts can we suffer. If our brother or any man does aught against us, it may be a sign that we have deserved it through some acts of our own; and he, through the evil in his nature, is but the medium of the Divine Law which punishes us for that which we have done before. And even so, if that is done against us which we have not deserved, then is the doer punished by his own acts, while we will be compensated through some means for the sorrow, the loss, or the pain that we may have suffered. Thus does the Divine Law punish or reward; and for this reason must we forgive those who do aught against us, understanding that the Divine Law will punish them for what they did, and reward us for that which has been done against us.

"Therefore is the kingdom of heaven likened unto a certain king, which would make a reckoning with his servants. And when he had begun to reckon, one was brought unto him, which owed him ten thousand talents. But forasmuch as he had not wherewith to pay, his lord commanded him to be sold, and his wife, and children and all that he had, and payment to be made. The servant therefore fell down and worshiped him, saying, Lord,

THE SON OF GOD

have patience with me, and I will pay thee all. And the lord of that servant, being moved with compassion, released him, and forgave him the debt.

"But the same servant went out, and found one of his fellow servants which owed him an hundred pence; and he laid hands on him, and took him by the throat, saying, Pay me that thou owest. So his fellow servant fell down at his feet and besought him, saying, Have patience with me, and I will pay thee all. And he would not; but went and cast him into prison, till he should pay the debt. So when his fellow servants saw what was done, they were very sorry, and came and told unto their lord all that was done. Then his lord called him unto him, and saith to him, Thou wicked servant, I forgave thee all that debt because thou desiredst me: Shouldest not thou also have had compassion on thy fellow servant, even as I had mercy on thee? And his lord was wroth, and delivered him to his tormentors, till he should pay all that was due unto him. So likewise shall my heavenly Father do also unto you, if ye from your hearts forgive not every one his brother their trespasses." Matt. 18:23-35.

No master could teach a greater truth, nor make it plainer than this. There is no qualification made as to whom we should forgive. He tells us plainly that we must forgive all, no matter who it may be, if we in turn wish to be forgiven.

There is no virtue in prayer to God which comes from the lips if we have not forgiveness in the heart. There is no virtue in telling our brother that we forgive him if the heart does not forgive. But if the heart forgives, if it has freed itself from all ill-feeling, all resentment, then have we truly forgiven those who did ill against us, even if we do not tell them so; for the virtue is not in the telling, but in the attitude of mind itself.

Jesus taught that all must forgive the wrongs committed against them, and that this forgiveness must be in the heart. This

THE SON OF GOD

means that we must free the heart from all ill-feeling, from all resentment; for ill-feeling and resentment are poisons which keep the soul in darkness, and which do not allow it to become free or illuminated. In this, is the power of hate and of resentment, that it keeps the soul bound, it does not allow it to find the light; and it is for this reason that no man can become the Son of God so long as there is hate or resentment or jealousy in the heart toward any being.

To be forgiven for any debt that we owe, does not free us from the debt; but it frees us from the act. It still remains a debt and must be paid; but with the paying of the debt the record is wiped clean. Whereas, if we are not forgiven for a wrong committed, even though we repay it, the record remains; therefore it is necessary for us to forgive trespasses even as we desire to be forgiven.

Before we can become Christie, before we can know God, before we can become the temple of the living God, we must have learned to forgive all men. Unless we do so, the conscience within, that still, small voice which is awakened when the soul is aroused to consciousness, will continue to accuse us and to condemn us; and there is no peace for man until he makes peace with his own conscience. One makes peace with one's conscience only by obeying it. The enlightened conscience teaches one the same thing that the master Jesus taught mankind centuries ago. Only personal pride prevents man from doing what is right; for our pride, that Satan of old, continually makes us believe that it lowers our dignity to forgive. The man with a clear conscience, free from accusations of wrong, does not recognize "dignity" unless it is in the right; for his dignity is the dignity of the Father, and is within and recognizes only the right.

"We know that we have passed out of death into life because we love the brethren. He that loveth not, abideth in death." John 3:14.

THE SON OF GOD

It is not faith in a creed, not the upholding of some special church that brings life; but it is living in harmony with the Divine Law that brings eternal life to man.

As man does this he awakens to the truth, and he lives according to the truth. He becomes the church, or the bride, of God; for in Him are all things. He is the temple; and, as God is within the temple, he worships within, not through a service that is of the lips only, but a service to which is dedicated the thoughts, the desires, and the acts. This is the true service.

No man being sufficient unto himself, but all men forming parts of a whole, it is well for men, even those who have reached Illumination, to be formed into an Association and to have symbolic buildings wherein they may meet and wherein, through an outer service, they may symbolize that which they have already found within, that which they have already become; but this is all that the external church can do.

To love our fellow man is to be willing to help him in every way possible. It means that our life will be one of service; and, through service, through love for our fellow-man, do we find eternal life, or that which we call Immortality of Soul. He that has love for his brother also has life. We need then simply to realize love in the heart for our fellowman in order to find life; and, as we find life, we will recognize that we are a part of the universal whole, that we are becoming the temples of the living God, and that, as we become perfect through our love, we become the Sons of God, we become Christs.

"Love is of God; and every one that loveth is begotten of God and knoweth God. He that loveth not knoweth not God; for God is Love." 1 John 4:7-8.

The beginning of true life is in love. Unless we love the truth we will not seek for the truth, and unless we seek it we will

THE SON OF GOD

not find it; and if we do not find it we cannot live it. The beginning of all things, whether of good or of evil, is in love. Love for the pleasures of the flesh will lead us into doing those things which will gratify the unhallowed love of the flesh, and therein is death. Love of the truth will lead us to do the things that will give us truth, and therein do we find life. Love is therefore at the foundation of all things. It is the beginning of life, as it is also the beginning of death.

"But whoso hath the world's goods, and seeth his brother have need, and shutteth up his bowels of compassion from him, how doth the love of God abide in him? My little children, let us not love in word, neither with the tongue, but in deed and in truth." 1 John 3:17-18.

Here we are taught the necessity of acting. Not that which we say counts, but that which we do. If we say that we love our brother and help him not in his need, then are we liars and the truth is not in us. Nevertheless, even though we confess not love for him in words, if we help him in his need, then do we express our love for him; for it is service that God desires and not words. Only by giving to others when they need, do we prove that we have the love of God in our hearts, and that we follow the divine command. This is religion, it is obedience to the Christ within. It is the building of the Divine Soul, that which is eternal.

And through such service did Jesus become the Son of God. But not he alone has become the Son of God. All men, through love and service to humanity, may become the only begotten Sons of the Father. He who can and does love has God within himself; and it is from this that the power comes to heal the sick and to do all manner of good.

"Ye are the temples of the living God" should be written in letters of fire above the doors of all places wherein man dwells. And to make this a fact it is only necessary that man should love

THE SON OF GOD

his fellow-man, that he should do as the Divine Law commands.

"God is love," and whoso loveth his brother has God within him. It thus follows that, if Christ is with the Father and God is in those who love, then we are to become living Christs the same as Jesus became through his love for mankind.

"God in me, and I in you." Man thus, if he follows the sacred teachings, becomes a Christ, the Son of God. "Love is of God: and every one that loveth is begotten of God and knoweth God." There is no qualification in this statement. He who loveth his fellowman and doeth accordingly, comes to know God, comes to have the Christie power within himself; for he is, in very truth, "the temple of the living God."

"No man hath beheld God at any time; if we love one another, God abideth in us." John 4:12.

No man can see God. The flesh can see and understand only that which is of the flesh. But if man obeys the Divine Law, if he thinks, desires, and acts in harmony with the Law; if he makes deliberate efforts for the finding of the Christ, then he gradually becomes the Son of God. He transmutes, or changes, the carnal self into the real Self. He changes the personality into the Individuality. And, when he has accomplished this, he is a conscious individual entity, he is become an Illuminated Soul, he can then see God, for he is become one with God. When he has become thus illuminated, when he has become the Conscious Individualized Soul, then is he truly the temple of the living God, and God dwells within the temple. Moreover, man has then become the Son of God, the Christ; and through this becoming will he have received the power possessed by Jesus who had also become the Christ through his love for humankind and through his thoughts, his desires, and his works.

"If a man say, I love God, and hateth his brother, he is a

THE SON OF GOD

liar: for he that loveth not his brother whom he hath seen cannot love God whom he hath not seen."

All true growth begins through faith in God and His law, and through works on the plane where one lives. Thus the man who desires to become the Son of God, the dynamic Christ, must begin his labors on the plane of being whereon he lives when the desire for the higher life comes to him. His first duty is to himself; for, only in the changing of the self, will he be able to show the change to others. He will be faithful to the work he has in hand no matter what may be its nature. If but a laborer in the fields he will perform his labor well and with patience, knowing that just as soon as he has become worthy, something greater will be ready for him to do. While performing his labor he will prepare himself for the greater work; and, the moment he is ready for it, the work will be given him to do. Only those things for which we are fitted will be given us to do. The attempt to do things for which we are not fitted, ends in failure.

Thus, as the Law reveals itself to us we try to obey it. With each attempt there will be greater power to do until in the end we have mastered even those things which seemed most difficult. We will love our fellowmen, even those that hate us, knowing that hate is of the flesh, of the carnal self; knowing that in hate there is sickness, sorrow, and death. Moreover, we know that the hate of another need in no wise affect us, but that it affects most of all him that hates. While the love we bear towards others has its effects directly upon ourselves, even though it is neither appreciated nor accepted by those whom we love.

Love is the Law; and through love do we come to do the service required of us in order to become that which we desire to be. In order to have the love of God within the soul, man must love all mankind. It is not possible for us to love God and hate our fellowman. There is no distinction of race, it is for us to feel kindly toward all mankind. We must believe in, and be in

THE SON OF GOD

sympathy with, universal man- kind; and, through this love and the fruits of this love, do we become the Sons of God.

There is no way except through love in the heart. Neither creed nor doctrine nor ritualism can give us God, nor make us the children of God. Only through love in the heart, which makes all things possible, can we come to know God, who Himself is all love. Through thoughts and desires, which end in deeds or acts, do we become Sons of God; and nowhere is there greater opportunity than in service to those who have less understanding of God than we have. For this reason did Jesus teach: "Inasmuch as ye have done it unto one of the least of these my brethren, ye have done it unto me."

God does not need our service personally; but his creation needs our service, and, when we give service, or help, to those whom he has created, we do it directly to Him. If we feed those who are an hungered and cannot obtain food, then we have done it to Him. If we feed those who are able to work and thereby obtain food, we do not His will; for then we weaken those who might become strong through the effort they themselves are able to make. "You have heard that it hath been said: An eye for an eye, and a tooth for a tooth; but I say unto you, Resist not him that is evil." Matt. 5:38-39.

To demand an eye for an eye, is to do to others that which they do to us. It means that we would give them just that which they give to us. If they slander us, we would slander them. If they hate us, we would hate them. If they commit wrong against us, we would do the same to them. This is not the Divine Law; for there is no virtue in giving a blow to him that gives a blow to us.

The Law is that we should give to others, not that which they give to us, but that which they should give us. "We need not concern ourselves with the acts of another, whether evil or otherwise. Our duty is ours alone; and, no matter what others do to

THE SON OF GOD

us, it is our duty to do only that which is good, for then we receive the good fruits of our good acts, while if we return evil for evil, we reap the reaction of our evil. Our acts therefore do not concern others at all, even though they do evil to us, for we have nothing to do with their actions. If we return in kind, we have gained nothing except possibly to punish them; but we reap the evil for the punishment given, and are the loser." We should remember the words of Jesus: "What is that to thee? Follow thou me."

Therefore we must not demand an eye for an eye, but return that which we ourselves would like to receive. Our whole duty is between ourselves and God, and consists in service to others, for only in service is there reward. Jesus everywhere taught his disciples not to resist him that is evil. He taught all men that God has said: "vengeance is mine, saith the Lord." This does not imply that God punishes the evil doer, nor that God seeks vengeance for the evil that we do; but the Divine Law, being just and absolute and always working, rewards each and every one according to his thoughts, his desires, and his acts. Not only this, but as the prayer is the answer, so is the deed the reward. Evil brings evil, goodness brings goodness, and therefore goodness is power.

God punishes no one. Man, through the reactionary effects of his own deeds, punishes or blesses himself. If aught comes to us which we consider evil, it may be accounted for by some act of ours which has set the Law into motion, which in its turn has brought to us the punishment, or that which we consider evil.

All men are therefore instruments of the Divine Law in the giving of just judgment. Just as the good man, through his works and his blessings, is the rewarder of the good, so is the evil man, through his evil deeds, the punisher of those who do evil. Law is one, it is the use of the Law that brings about the different results.

Jesus taught that he who has not taken up the cross has not

THE SON OF GOD

renounced all and cannot be his disciple: that is to say, no one is qualified to follow the Christ unless he is prepared to give up the unworthy desires of the flesh for those of the soul, and to take the consequences of such renunciation. For no one can follow the Christ who is not willing to obey the Divine Law and to exchange his carnal, material life for the higher life.

"Resist not evil," means just what it says. It means that we should never employ force, never compel another to do that which he does not wish to do, never do anything that is contrary to love; and, if men still continue to do evil towards us we should put up with their offense, forget that they are trying to injure us, and go our way. The law of non-resistance to evil, or the refusal to recognize evil, unites all the teachings of Jesus into one harmonious whole; not, however, when it is considered simply as a creed or a doctrine, but when we recognize it as an absolute Law, a principle that must be obeyed if we desire to reap the benefits of the Law.

It is impossible to resist evil, to fight against those who are opposed to us, and at the same time to follow the great command: "Love thy brother, for whoso loveth his brother has God in him; for God is love." We cannot fight with a man and take his life, and still love him. That which we love we do not attempt to destroy, we cherish it, we try to keep it from destruction and even give ourselves so that the loved one may live.

"Ye have heard that it was said, Thou shalt love thy neighbor and hate thine enemy (Lev. 19:17-18). But I say unto you: Love your enemy, and pray for them that persecute you; for he maketh his sun to rise on the evil and the good, and sendeth rain on the just and the unjust. For if ye love them that love you, what reward have ye? Do not even the publicans the same? And if ye salute your brethren only, what do ye more than others? Do not even the Gentiles the same? Ye therefore shall be perfect, as your heavenly Father is perfect."

THE SON OF GOD

In this we have the Law; for, if we have mastered the evil in us so that we love our enemies as we are commanded, we will no longer wish to resist him that is evil. We will love all, knowing that each does only that which he understands to be for his own good. The Father who is the Creator does not withhold the sunshine from those who are evil, and give it only to those who are good. He allows the sun to shine upon all. His it is not to punish but to give. He knows that men are continually punishing themselves through their evil thoughts and deeds. He knows that they are living in eternal torment all the day, that the conscience gives them neither peace nor rest nor contentment; and for this reason he neither curses, punishes, nor destroys. But the Law allows men's deeds to bring their own results. The sowing is the reaping.

Awakening man, who is trying to become like the Father, who is seeking the way to Divine Illumination and to Sonship, must do like the Father; for only in this way can we become like Him. For this reason, the man who is truly seeking "the truth, the way, and the life," will not resist evil; he will pray for them that persecute him just as the Father sends the sunshine even upon those that are indifferent to Him.

If we love only those that love us and that are kind to us, we do not more than the most degraded of humankind is doing. Even the most hardened criminal has a sort of love, an affection for those of his own kind who show kindness to him. If we want to become men of power, Sons of God, we must show love and kindness to all, even those who do us injury, even as the Father sends the rain to those who are ungrateful.

To hate an enemy will not make him better, nor yet will it free us from his hatred and his persecution. But if we refuse to receive the hatred, if we give love in exchange for the hatred, then will we receive the blessings of love; and our love to such will be like coals of fire, searing into the conscience and allowing them no

THE SON OF GOD

rest until they discontinue their persecution. The first commandment is: "Be at peace with all men." Consider no man as insignificant or foolish. If peace be destroyed, strive to reestablish it with all your strength. The service of Cod is the destruction of enmity. "Know that all men are brothers and sons of the one God; break peace with no man."

"Be ye merciful, even as your Father is merciful." To be like the Father, we must do as the Father does; for this reason, we must show mercy to all men. Those who hate do so because they think they have a reason for so doing, and because they know no better way by which to protect themselves. They are as yet slaves to themselves, and do not understand the Divine Law; otherwise, they would know that no one except themselves can bring harm to them. "Judge not, and ye shall not be judged: and condemn not, and ye shall not be condemned." Luke 6:37-49.

We have no right to judge our fellowmen harshly; for we know not what cause they may have for their actions. It is ours to forgive, it is not ours to judge. No man has a right to hold the acts of another in judgment, even when his acts are clearly wrong. The action of a man is only between himself and his God, unless he interferes with the liberties of others; in such a case, protective methods must be taken by society. We have only to watch our own actions, our own thoughts, and our own deeds. The Divine Law takes care of that which others do, as it takes care of that which we do. Each one must therefore deal directly with the Law and not through the medium of another; for this reason, we can no more judge another than another can judge us.

But if we do judge, then is that judgment written against us by the Divine Law the same as all our other acts; and with the judgment by which we judge others we also will be judged. For this reason, "Judge not," lest by the same judgment ye be judged.

Jesus was careful to enjoin all men to forgive others, that

they might have their own trespasses forgiven. This idea he repeated many times. It follows, then, that every man before bringing his offering of prayer is required to pardon all trespasses. If he does not the offering is acceptable neither to God nor to his own conscience; for it is not given in love. Only thoughts created in love are acceptable to the soul; and, only through thoughts, desires, and acts that have their beginning in love, can the soul become illuminated.

In James 4:11, are found these words: "Speak not evil one of another, brethren. He that speaketh against a brother, or judgeth his brother, speaketh against the law; but if thou judgest the law, thou art not a doer of the law, but a judge. One only is the lawgiver and judge, even he who is able to save and destroy; but who art thou that judgest thy neighbor?"

The Divine Law is above all men, and yet all men are bound by the Law. The Law has a judge which is he who gave it; and no one else has the right either to judge or to interfere with it. As we are all equally bound by the Law, and as the Law is absolutely just, and judges each one according to his thoughts, desires, and deeds, and rewards accordingly, no man has a right to interfere with it; and to do so results in a just punishment.

"My brethren, hold not the faith of our Lord Jesus Christ, the Lord of glory, with respect to persons. For if there come into your synagogues a man with a gold ring, in fine clothing; and ye have regard to him that weareth the fine clothing, and say, Sit thou here in a good place; and ye say to the poor man, Sit thou here, or sit under my footstool; are ye not divided in your own mind? And become judges with evil thoughts? Harken, my beloved brethren, did not God choose them that are poor as to the world, to be rich in faith, and heirs to the kingdom which he promised to them that love him. But ye have dishonored the poor man. Do not the rich among you oppress you, and themselves drag you before the judgment-seats? Do not they blaspheme the honorable name by

THE SON OF GOD

which ye are called. Howbeit if ye fulfill the royal law according to the Scripture, Thou shalt love thy neighbor as thyself, ye do well; but if ye have respect of persons, ye commit sin, being convicted by the law as transgressors. For whosoever shall keep the whole law, and yet stumble in one point, he is become guilty of all. For he that said, Do not commit adultery, also said, Do not kill. Now if thou dost not commit adultery, but killest, thou art become a transgressor of the law. So speak ye, and so do, as men that are to be judged by a. law of liberty. For judgment is without mercy to him that hath showed no mercy: mercy glorieth against judgment."

God does not respect the person. The person is the personality, it is only the shell of that which is within. God does not look to see whether we wear rings of gold or whether our clothing is of the best material and the most fashionable cut; for these features belong to the person, that which is not lasting. God looks upon the man, that which is interior, that which is going on within. He looks upon the thoughts, upon the desires, and upon the acts of man. A man may be poor in worldly goods, but if he entertains clean thoughts and desires, if his efforts are for the accomplishment of the work for which he came to earth, if he is therefore changing the personality into the individuality, or the Soul- such a man is the one that is acceptable to God. Even though a man may wear the most fashionable apparel, jewels of gold and diamonds, even though his intellect may be mighty, yet, if his heart is dark with evil and if he neither knows nor cares for the Divine Law, such a man does not know God.

Nor are these things evil in themselves. Gold and jewels and fine clothing are not to be condemned; but when the effort to obtain them requires time and thought which should be given to the real things of life, then do they become evil and destructive to all that is eternal.

God recognizes not the personality, no matter how beautiful it may be, because the personality is connected only with

THE SON OF GOD

the body, it is that which came from the earth and that which must return again to the earth, losing every vestige of its identity as it passes from one state to the other. But the individuality is that which is of the Father; for it becomes like the Father, it is the Christ, the Son of God.

"Except your righteousness shall exceed the righteousness of the scribes and Pharisees, ye shall in no wise enter into the kingdom of heaven." Matt. 5:20.

The righteousness of the scribes and Pharisees, what was it? The scribes and Pharisees were devoted members of the synagogue, they were faithful in their attendance at the services. They dressed well, they glorified the personality, they upheld the written law. In most cases, the law was man-made, it was in harmony with things man considered right. Being men who lived the carnal life, the life that is ruled by the flesh, they did not understand the Divine Law.

Such were the Pharisees, they knew nothing of God, because the personality, being of the earth, cannot know God. Men who are like the scribes and the Pharisees are denied the kingdom of God. Instead of giving service to God with his words, man must give service to God through his acts. Instead of fine clothing, he must perform fine deeds, and therefore erect a fine temple. Instead of glorifying the personality, man must transmute, change, the personality into the individuality. He must know the Divine Law, and above all else, he must make deliberate efforts to live in harmony with the Divine Law and to reach the state called Soul Consciousness, or Oneness with the Father. Not merely through faith and faithful attendance upon a church, is Sonship possible; but, only through obedience to the Divine Law, can man become the Son of God.

THE END

THE SON OF GOD

THE TEMPLE OF THE ILLUMINATI

The Temple of the Illuminati is not a secret order in the same sense as the Masons, the Odd Fellows, or the Templars. It is, rather, more like the old Essenean Fraternity, a School of Spirituality, a School of, or for, aspiring Souls- Souls that are no longer satisfied with the things of the carnal self, hut desire to know, to be, and to do.

As the name indicates, the Temple of the Illuminati is a Fraternity, or Brotherhood, of those who have passed through certain stages of growth and have attained such a degree of enlightenment that they desire further instructions which will help them to attain Illumination of Soul, or At-one-ment with God, the Father.

In many Fraternities, Initiation means nothing more than the ceremonial rites attendant upon the reception of members. It may possibly signify a required amount of instruction that has been given the candidate, with little regard to his understanding or appropriation of such instruction. In the Temple of the Illuminati, the strongest emphasis is placed on the importance of the stages, or degrees, of growth which the candidate has actually experienced, as a result of instructions received.

Thus, in this Fraternity, outer initiation is only a symbolization, or emblematic representation, of the degree of understanding that the candidate is to attain, or that he has already attained, in his growth. In this Fraternity, the inner growth is promoted by following clearly outlined instructions and by the use of Sacred Mantrams.

There is an outer organized Brotherhood of the Temple of the Illuminati. However, the members of the Inner Brotherhood, those who have received the instructions, who have followed the

THE SON OF GOD

Sacred Mantrams, greatly outnumber those of the outer; in other words, many are eligible to membership who have not been privileged to be present at a Convocation and to receive the conferring of degrees. They are eligible to membership in that they have received the prescribed instructions concerning Soul Illumination, and have given satisfactory evidence of sincerity and devotion in trying to live a life that harmonizes with these instructions; but, for some reason, they have been unable to be present at one of the Convocations.

In so far as possible for them to do so, all worthy seekers are encouraged to become affiliated with a Temple organization. Such fellowship as a Fraternity affords, does much to strengthen one in one's purpose, to stimulate one to one's best endeavors, and to quicken one's ambition in all good works; while the ceremonial features of Initiation, when understood in their symbolic significance, constitute a most impressive and sublime ritual.

However, to the isolated members of the Temple of the Illuminati, who are not privileged to enjoy such fellowship and to be the recipients of such impressive rites, let this message be made plain"

"True Initiation is a process of growth, it is a refining process, it is a purifying process, by means of which the soul becomes more Christ-like in all its qualities; therefore, that which is vital and fundamental in initiation one may experience in his own consciousness, no matter how isolated his life may be. Furthermore, no matter how many degrees one may have received through the outer ritual, unless one has attained correct understanding of truth, and has experienced the proper purification of heart, and the consequent proportionate degree of Illumination of Soul, one has not passed through the true Initiation." The systems of instruction given under the auspices of the Temple of the Illuminati receive the general names, Soul Science, Soul Science and Success, or Soul Science and Immortality. Each name

THE SON OF GOD

emphasizes one particular feature of the purpose attained through its study and its practice. The instructions in general have for their aim the harmonious development of the complete man, body, mind, and soul. This is brought about through proper understanding of the divine laws, and through the use of Sacred Mantrams.

The special object of these teachings is to fit all aspirants, through knowledge wisely used, not only to be masters of their own lives and conditions, but to help their weaker brothers in the one family of God, whose home is the universe. Purity of motive, thought, and life; holy use of holy gifts; justice and fairness in all dealings; sympathy and brotherly love; in short, truth practiced- these are a few of the stones gathered for the foundation of the Temple.

The faithful aspirant giving himself with pure motives and determined purpose to the pursuit and practice of the methods and teachings set forth, will, of a surety, unfold the inherent powers of the Soul; such as, gifts of healing, intuition, discernment, and spiritual understanding. No distinction of sex is recognized. Man and woman possessing a sincere heart and a willing mind and upright character alike are eligible to membership.

In the fullness of time, retreats will be established where the sick and sorrow-tossed may go for healing, rest, and instructions. In the cities, circles will be formed for all manner of practical work. The ministry of healing will be offered whenever possible under the guidance of regular physicians who have also received training in Soul Science and Soul Culture. Especially is it desired that tender sympathy and ministry shall be given to all the so-called outcast, or fallen man or woman, and that every member of the Temple shall consider himself a Good Samaritan, ready to do, to dare, and to suffer, if need be, in order to save his weaker brother.

THE SON OF GOD

The work and the principles of the Temple of the Illuminati are such as to insure opportunity for Mystic connection through membership in the Order with the most advanced and spiritual minds of past ages and of the present age; also, through their teachings, exoteric and esoteric, one receives such instructions as will develop the highest powers of the soul, and at the same time open the field for consecrated and useful service and activity. It should be emphasized that the mission of the Temple is to teach those who come into touch with it. Teachers connected with the Temple may be equal to those who would be called "Masters," or "Mahatmas," by Occult Fraternities. But the Temple of the Illuminati does not put them forth as such; they are ranked only in the role of teachers, or instructors.

The teachings must necessarily be general, intended to enlighten as well as to arouse the conscience, in order that the aspirant may become self-reliant in his choices and in his decisions. The purpose is to give such clear exposition of the Divine Law that the student may learn to determine beforehand the reactionary effects of thought and deed, and thus be led to choose the right.

It is intended that the fundamental laws of the Christ shall be taught, and how to live in harmony with them. The goal in mind for the students is to become masters themselves of themselves, rather than to come under the control of a master. All powers, all mastership, all divinity, comes from within, from the Soul, from the Center of the Being. The teacher can only direct the student to the path that leads to Illumination of Soul. But the student must travel the path and must do the work for himself. However, by persistent effort the student may become even as the teacher and possibly even greater. Not slavery does the Temple teach, but freedom from slavery; mastership over conditions, not bondage under conditions. Obedience to the spirit of the teachings is necessary; for no one can learn the deeper truth except through obedience to the truth he already has. Knowledge of deific things

THE SON OF GOD

is the result of growth of Soul; and growth of Soul is the result of faithful obedience to the Divine Law in its various aspects in all departments of life.

To the seeker who has made up his mind to live the true life, the thing that looks like an impossible barrier to Sonship and Illumination is the memory of the past; for the memory of his past life comes before him again and again to discourage him. Concerning this it is fitting to quote from a poet unknown in name:

> "All the past things are past and over,
> The tasks are done and the tears are shed.
> Yesterday's errors let yesterday cover;
> Yesterday's wounds, which smart and bled,
> Are healed with the healing that night has shed."

To let the dead bury their dead, and to follow the Christ, is the hardest lesson the student has to learn. To give up the old and all that it held; to follow the new with all that it shall hold for us- this, the hardest task of all, becomes the Giver of Life and Light and Immortality.

It is to be clearly understood that no one can receive the Temple Degree- Knight of the Rose and Cross- who has not at least taken the first year's instructions in Soul Science, and who does not possess the text-books that form a part of the instructions.

A chain can be only as strong as its weakest link, and an Order can be of greatest service only when its members understand the laws of which each member is to make use in his service to humankind. If there is but one member who is ignorant of these laws, the whole Fraternity will be judged by the ignorance of that member, and its services will be appreciated accordingly.

THE SON OF GOD

SOUL SCIENCE

Soul Science is the science that teaches equal development of the physical, the mental, and that which concerns the soul, giving perfect balance and harmony in their culture.

Soul Science is not simply a religion. It is a Science-Philosophy-Religion; and it is in perfect harmony with the teachings of Jesus, the great Master. It is founded not on theory, but on facts- material, tangible facts- the teachings of the Masters, proved true and scientific, and applicable and practical, time and time again.

Mind is mortal and dies with the body; but that which the mind builds- the Soul- lives on through eternity. This power, which the mind is able to build, and which we recognize as the Soul, is the greatest power man can know- a power that is a thousand times greater than the mind.

The power of the Soul can be used to regain health when you are ill, to maintain it when you are well and strong; to heal others, in fact, to attain perfect development and to gain success in every branch of endeavor, if you know how to use it. Soul Science teaches how to use it. It teaches even how the poverty-stricken man can rise above his conditions, and become a success in the business world, and a credit to himself and to his God. It teaches the unhappy how to become happy.

THE NAME

As the name, Soul Science, indicates, the teaching is, primarily, the science of Soul Illumination, or the science of the Soul: it unfolds and interprets the laws and the principles underlying the growth, the culture, and the training of soul powers. Every science implies its corresponding art. These instructions,

THE SON OF GOD

when applied, become the finest of fine arts- the art of the interpretation of truth; the art of the application of truth to human needs; the art of cultivating and encouraging the most delicate graces of heart, the most subtle uses of thought power, the most refined touches and imaginings of consciousness; the art of "righteous judgment;" the art of putting a kind interpretation on the deeds of others; in short, the art of the Christ-life. They become an art that constantly lures one on to perfection- a perfection, however, that as constantly evades and escapes one's grasp; yet, with every escape, it lures the more enticingly. The science and the art of illumination must go hand in hand: the one giving a clear understanding of the laws of truth, the other making practical application of these laws to the needs of life.

SOUL SCIENCE AND SUCCESS

The title, Soul Science and Success, emphasizes the principle that culture of soul leads to success. It is based on the conviction that success is secured through the intelligent direction of well-trained thought powers. True success is a practical application of the law: "Seek ye first the kingdom of God and his righteousness, and all these things will be added unto you." In this, it is to be understood that the kingdom of God means the establishment of love, truth, and justice in the thought-kingdom of man's consciousness. In proportion as these divine qualities have become the actuating principle of a man's thought-life, in that proportion has he reached the vibrations of true success. Acceptable, worthy service attracts its corresponding reward. The inculcation, in a person's nature, of the qualities of love, truth, and justice, and the intelligent direction of well-trained thought powers, will increase his efficiency in whatever profession he may serve; thus, through the study and the practice of Soul Science principles, an ever-increasing success is assured him.

THE SON OF GOD

SOUL SCIENCE AND IMMORTALITY

The designation, Soul Science and Immortality, is also given to this system of instructions. The significance of this name is due to the fact that Soul is the only immortal part of man's nature, and that Illumination of Soul leads to Conscious Immortality. At the transition period known as death, the body returns to the great storehouse of elements whence it came; the spirit, or life-principle, returns to the universal storehouse of spirit, or universal life, whence it came; the mind does not continue as an individual entity; whereas, the soul is that part of man's being that continues to exist. Its existence may be of various stages: as, it may exist in a chaotic state, little more than a crude mingling of good and evil; or, it may be in the primitive stages of a nucleus, in which the good is beginning to take more or less definite shape and to act as a transmuting influence over the evil; or, it may have reached an advanced stage of purification such that it is a well-formed center of light, pure and radiant. Thus, "the light that lighteth all the world" has become individualized and self-existent. When the soul has become a nucleus of light it has become an immortal entity. This is the true illumination, this is immortality of soul. From this, it is seen that immortality of soul is not something thrust upon mankind, whether he will or no, that it is not an inevitable fate which man is destined to meet, regardless of his own choice; but rather is it true that immortality of soul is something to be attained, something in the attainment of which man may have conscious part and free choice. The stage of development known as Immortality of Soul is a goal aimed at in the Soul Science instructions.

SOUL SCIENCE TELLS HOW

The Philosophy of Soul Science shows how a soul can be built, or developed. It shows how such graces and such powers of soul as one desires can be developed. You are told how to meet

THE SON OF GOD

success in the financial world and how to draw things to you that you need and desire. This is to be done not through exercising control over others, but by increasing one's own efficiency in rendering service to others. No point needs more clear and explicit emphasis than the fact that Soul Science does not countenance any phase of hypnotic control, or mastery, over others in order to bring benefit to oneself. Soul Science stands for the cultivation of the self and of mastery over one's own self. Soul Science always and forever stands for the principle that success is to be attained through an exercise of one's own inner powers and resources in channels of usefulness to humanity; that success is to be attained through an increase of proficiency and competency in some line of service. Soul Science teaches how to cultivate one's resources and how to increase one's proficiency and competency. It stands on the principle of thoroughness, and makes use of no "success-in-a-day" method of instruction.

The mission of Soul Science is Unity. You can believe in any religion you desire, and still accept every word of Soul Science. Its predominating mission is to show humanity that the Great Teacher is here now, ready and willing to help you find the Christ at his second coming- the present.

This is the only Philosophy that will help you in all conditions of life, as it equally develops all the elements of physical, mental, and spiritual existence. Development along one line to the neglect of others would make of you a physical, mental, or moral cripple. Your happiness demands good health, a prosperous business, harmonious social conditions, and a sane understanding of a true Philosophy or Religion. All these desirable and necessary things will be yours when you understand Soul Science Philosophy, and when your Soul becomes strong enough to control your thoughts in the midst of life's affairs.

The Great Law is that the desire within us to do a certain thing or to accomplish a noble and worthy purpose in life is proof

THE SON OF GOD

that we have the capacity to do that very thing. We may not be able to do them at this very minute. We doubtless need to cultivate and to develop the powers and the energies with which to accomplish. But, in time, through persistent and faithful effort, it is ours to accomplish, to achieve, to attain, to dare, to do. It is our sacred duty to realize our highest ideals, and to recognize and develop to the utmost the powers, forces, and energies latent within us. This is the mission of Soul Science- to show the student how to awaken and arouse from the sleep of latency the manifold resources of his own being.

The time is past for men, and especially women, to sit down with folded hands and wait for things to come to them- things which may never come without the exercise of great Soul Power. You perhaps feel that you possess a power, a force, which, if you could but learn its proper use, would help you to achieve the things you desire. It is the development of this power that we teach, in order that you may fulfill your deepest desires.

THE POWER OF THOUGHT

If you fully understood the power of Thought Force, its laws, its principles, its might; and if you were proficient in directing Thought Force in harmony with a correct under- standing of its laws- then, you would be able to dissolve the earth by a single thought and to create another world by another thought. This is not to say, however, that expenditure of Thought Force in channels of demonstration and display is under any circumstances to be encouraged. This is merely a statement of fact concerning the possibilities of Thought Force in the hands of one who is in reality an Adept in its use. Nevertheless, it is to be emphasized that the true Adept is guided and guarded against the possibility of making harmful use of Thought Force. Under all conditions he will use the power only for good and worthy purposes. An Adept is one who has full, complete, and remarkable use of Thought Force. Yet, there is no room for discouragement in the belief that you cannot

THE SON OF GOD

become an Adept. Even a limited knowledge of the laws of thought, together with the power of thought control, which is gained through Soul Development, will enable you to gratify every worthy ambition.

This "Magic of Mind" has been proved time and again to be most powerful for directing things in the way man wishes them to be. It has been said that mind is all; but this statement is not true. Mind simply acts as a builder; and unless man builds Soul, all dies with the body, and the opportunity for an eternally existing Soul is lost for that particular lifetime.

Thought being thus powerful, how much more powerful must be the Soul that has been builded by a mind that understands the laws, principles, and powers of thought! Thinking creative thoughts, forming habits of constructive and wholesome thought, awakening the Soul from its long sleep of latency, is the true method for obtaining power; and, if this is accomplished in the right way, such a Soul, built in such a way, is eternal.

ALL RESTS WITHIN YOU

Your body, your environments, your finances, your opportunity, are all of your own making. In order to make them according to your truest desires and loftiest ambitions, it is necessary to know the Great Laws. The Master Jesus taught that he who had awakened and developed the Soul should have all needful things. Soul Science Philosophy tells how to develop- to awaken- to find- the Soul. Being potentially a Son of the living God, these things are yours by divine right. If you do not understand them, whose fault is it? You cannot blame your fellowman. You cannot blame your Creator. Then who is to blame?

Man was born potentially a creator, after the likeness of God, the Creator of all things. Jesus taught that the things he did

THE SON OF GOD

we could do also. Even more, he told us plainly that greater things we should do. You are, in degree, a creator now. Though not understanding the laws of creative thought, it may be that you are creating for yourself misery, failure, and sorrow; for perhaps you are reversing the great laws.

Do you know that you have the power to make yourself what you will? It rests with you whether you become a success or a failure. Success in all things lies within the palms of your hands, if you but know the laws that control body, mind, and soul. It is the knowledge of these Great Laws that the Soul Science Philosophy teaches. To follow the instructions requires very little formal or verbal faith; for when the student obeys the laws, results must become manifest. There can be no failure, if one gives persistent, honest, faithful, conscientious attention to the task of Soul Development. As in working at the building of a house, if the plans are correct, results are sure. Made in the image of God and endowed with god-like qualities, man contains the spark or germ of Godhood within his nature. It needs but the proper development of this spark of divinity to attain health, prosperity, and happiness; for these are his birthright by divine decree. Had man alone been the one who decreed, it might have been different; but it was God Himself who made the divine decree and made man in His own image.

Man's Soul is a mighty Magnetic Force. It attracts or draws to it that which it likes, repelling that which it dislikes.

DEMAND FOR PROPER TEACHERS

The prejudices of the past centuries are being swept away. Never in the world's history has there been such a demand for true teachers. The time has come when workers are needed. The field is large and the workers are few. The Soul cannot advance unless it is active. It must have the chance to accumulate force from the planes of those who have achieved great Soulual knowledge and

THE SON OF GOD

development. It cannot advance if it slumbers any more than man can exist without working. The world is actually starving for the truth. There are many who are hungry, thirsty, seeking paths of light; and we must reach them.

The Masters of all ages are with us, lending us strength and power; for the time has come for a great change in the religious world. The Messiah is here and the world knows it not. He has come again even unto his own, but his own know it not. It is necessary to send out Messengers of Truth, to band all together in one complete bond ,of unity. Souls are worth more than all else; for through powers and energies and potencies of Soul can all things be achieved.

Not only should you enroll for your own success, but to enable you to become the helper and the healer of others. Millions are ready and waiting. Your friends who are sick, discouraged, and in sorrow will be only too glad to grasp at the life-line that you may throw them.

THE INSTRUCTIONS

The Preliminary Course in Soul Science, covering the first year's work, includes one typewritten lesson a week, and the following books:

"Soul Science, the Way to Immortality,"

"Christhood,"

"The Illuminated Faith,"

"The Divine Law."

A nominal fee of twenty-five dollars is asked for the first year to cover the cost of printing the text-books, the lessons, etc.

THE SON OF GOD

Of this amount, a small percentage goes to each teacher in the field for living expenses. The healing work connected with this school is free. Contributions are thankfully received and are used in furthering the great work. The whole privileges of the temple are included in the above.

SECOND YEARS WORK

Beginning with the second year, the lessons are semi-monthly. This is for the reason that each lesson contains, besides instructions concerning some aspect of the Divine Law, a Sacred Mantram, which, if followed by the student, will help him or her toward Illumination of Soul. Best results are obtained by using the same Mantram two weeks or longer.

The text-book included in this course is "The Christic Interpretation of the Gospel of St. John."

A nominal charge of $12.50 is made for the second year's instructions, including text-book and privilege of personal letters of instruction. Contributions toward the work are also received, which help to keep up the work.

THIRD YEARS WORK

The work for the third and last year is a continuation of the second year's work, leading the student more and more toward Illumination of Soul, or Soul Consciousness, through the use of Sacred Mantrams.

The text-book for this year is "Christisis." A nominal return of $12.50 is asked for the third year's instructions, including text-book and privilege of personal help through correspondence. Contributions toward the cause are gratefully received, which help to extend the work.

THE SON OF GOD

THREE YEARS' COURSE

If they so desire, students may enroll for the entire three years' course. In this case, a nominal charge of forty-five dollars is made for the entire instructions, which includes all books listed in the catalog of books following this announcement.

THE TEMPLE OF ILLUMINATION

The Temple of Illumination is the great outer body of the Temple of the Illuminati. It is the outer circle, an organization of kindred souls, who are interested in the truth, who want a pure and illuminated religion, but who do not desire to go deeply into any religious or philosophical training.

Each age demands a distinctive type of interpretation of truth, adapted to the requirements of that particular period of history. Truth is ever the same. Divine Laws have not changed since the beginning of time. But the world of thought advances; and each outgoing cycle requires a laying aside of its cloak, as the snake sheds its skin, that the incoming cycle may be "clothed upon" with a new garment, better suited to its needs. The texture and the designs and the coloring of the cloak of thought are determined by the particular emphasis that a given age employs in the interpretation of truth. For the human race to be enriched by all the varied aspects that truth and its realization may assume, it is necessary for the cloak of interpretation to be doffed and donned, again and again, in accordance with the laws of progress; it is necessary for a new system of emphasis in the interpretation of truth to be formulated from time to time.

The doffing of an old interpretation and the donning of a new mark a transition period that is attended by unsettledness of mind and by perplexity of thought. It is truly a period of stress and strain. The world of religions ideas is now in a transitional stage.

THE SON OF GOD

To satisfy this need, the Temple of Illumination offers a new system of interpretation- an interpretation that claims to be the natural outgrowth of the cyclic stages through which the world has already passed. The law of cyclic changes indicates that the time is ripe for a re-statement of religious principles, for a new presentation of fundamental laws. The unrest and the hunger of the present transitional stage of thought demands a different placing of emphasis in respect to the essentials of truth.

The religious thought of the past few centuries has been largely characterized by faith and belief. In respect to the teachings of Jesus, the Christ of the first century, the race-conception of truth has been passing through the period of childhood and early youth. Childhood is marked particularly by faith. The child has faith in his father. The child believes in his father's works and in his principles. When young manhood is attained, he is no longer satisfied with mere belief: he must demonstrate his faith by executing ideals; he must do such works as his father does. As a young man, he still has faith in his father; but his faith now demands the opportunity to exercise its own powers and to accomplish its own works. Religious teachings in the past has been largely occupied in the effort to convince mankind of the Messiahship of Jesus, and to establish the claims of the Christ. But mere belief does not long satisfy. "Faith without works is dead" is something more than a trite saying. It is a law of growth that faith must demonstrate its powers; it must work out its principles; it must execute; it must create. The incoming age should be one that is characterized by the power of intelligent faith, one that executes ideals in harmony with a faith that understands divine law.

A clear distinction should be made between blind faith and intelligent, or a seeing, faith; between a faith that is passive and a faith that is active; between an inert and a living faith; between faith in a personality and faith in a principle, faith in a Jesus and faith in the Christ. Jesus is the name of a man, a personality. The

THE SON OF GOD

Christ is the name of the Illumined Soul of Jesus. Jesus, as an historic character, lived his earth life, and passed out of the plane of manifestation. The Christ, as a divine principle developed and individualized in Jesus, is eternal; as an Illumined Soul, the Christ is immortal. Faith in Jesus, as a personality merely, is a blind faith. Faith in the Christ, as a state of consciousness that all may attain by living the teachings of Jesus and by obeying the law of love he demonstrated, is an intelligent faith.

To meet the need of the age in its demand for an interpretation of the laws of the spiritual kingdom, is one purpose of the Church of Illumination. That it is possible for man to understand and that it is necessary for him to understand in order that he may intelligently obey the law and live a life in harmony with it, is a settled conviction among leaders of religious thought today.

That Immortality of Soul is attainable is a fundamental doctrine of the Temple of Illumination. Immortality of Soul, however, is not thought of as something that is thrust on all alike, regardless of their desire or their seeking. It is not an inevitable factor of existence. The positive law of goodness functioning in the lives of men leads to Immortality of Soul, or to Soul Consciousness. In each life is a spark, or a germ, of the divine nature. This divine spark is the potential Christ, or the potential individual Soul, of that life. This may be nurtured and fed until it becomes "the light that lighteth all the world" of man's consciousness. When man becomes conscious of this light within his own Being, when he recognizes and obeys its "still, small voice," he has reached the state called Illumination of Soul, or Immortality; or, to express the same thought differently, he has reached the plane of Soul Consciousness.

The divine spark latent in each, individual may become a well-formed center of pure, white light. It may become a dynamic nucleus of fire- the Fire of Love, the Light of Truth. This fact

THE SON OF GOD

gives the key to the significance of the. name, Temple of Illumination. The name signifies that each individual is capable of becoming a center of illumination. Man is the Temple of Illumination, the Temple of the living Christ. Man is the architect of the temple of Solomon, which is a spiritual structure. The purified love of his own heart and the clarified understanding of his own soul become the altar-fire of this temple. This flame unconsciously radiates its light of understanding and its warmth of love and "good- will toward men."

The Temple of Illumination does not point to a heaven that awaits the faithful in the hereafter nor to a hell that reserves its torments for the wicked in the beyond, nor does it picture God as a personal judge of right and wrong. Heaven and hell are states of consciousness that begin here and now. Adjustments, results, and consequences are not postponed to a future life; they begin in the present and continue until satisfaction is made. Man's conscience, the God within, the Soul, is judge. Man will never find, nor will he need, a more exacting and severe judge than his own conscience; when its verdict has released him he is released indeed.

The will of God is supreme in the universe, operating directly or indirectly through the Hierarchies of angelic and ethereal forces and agencies. The Divine Will manifests its supremacy through the operation of natural laws, rather than by direct and personal control or interference. The superiority of the Divine Will, manifesting itself in the natural functioning of laws rather than by specific control, finds its necessary corollary in the individual responsibility of man. Man is responsible for becoming an intelligent channel for the functioning of divine law. The degree of man's ascent toward the divine image in which he was created, is determined by the degree of his understanding of these laws and their natural operation, and of his ability to live in harmony with them, and, consciously or unconsciously, to direct and to use them for the betterment of the world in which he is placed. He recognizes in the One Spirit, the Fatherhood of God; and, in

THE SON OF GOD

proportion as he lives in accord with the divine purpose, does he testify by his life to a practical recognition of the Brotherhood of Man.

The most important of the principles emphasized by the Temple of Illumination may be re-stated and condensed as follows:

Although the Will of God is supreme in the universe, its supremacy is manifested by the operation of impersonal and impartial law and by a system of hierarchial ministry, rather than by specific control.

The divine law of justice manifests itself in the absolute operation of the principle of cause and effect; thus, reward and punishment are natural consequences resulting from the operation of forces set into motion by individual or collective agencies.

Since all things are created by God and all human powers are endowed by Him, they are, in themselves, good; but, through ignorance or through a perverted disposition, man may misuse his inherent powers, and thus cause evil.

Being made in the image of God and being potentially an epitome of the universe, it is intended that, through the process of salvation, or regeneration, man should cultivate his inherent qualities until he attains the state of Christhood, or Illumination of Soul, or Individual Immortality- a state that indicates the entrance into a higher plane of consciousness and usefulness.

But, being honored with the right of choice, it is possible for man, through continued, persistent wrong doing and wrong thinking, to diffuse and to disintegrate his powers of soul to such an extent that individual immortality is unattainable. The cyclic wave of progress demands for this age an interpretation of the Law that enabled Jesus to bring into conscious expression His own

THE SON OF GOD

Christhood, or Sonship with God. The faith of the age demands a testing of the Christ Principles, and a verification, in individual consciousness, of the Christ-claim for man: "Ye are the temples of the living God;" and "Greater things than these shall ye do."

THE CHRISTIC INTERPRETATION AND MYSTIC CHRISTIANITY

The Christie Interpretation and Mystic Christianity are a part of the Temple of Illumination; they refer to the teaching of a religion that is free from iron-clad dogmas and fettering creeds, they aim at unity and true brotherhood.

Christic Interpretation, or Mystic Christianity, encourages freedom of individual conscience and freedom of investigation. It claims to be a science and a philosophy as well as a religion. It bases its claims as a religion on these facts: that it interprets God and truth to human nature; that it speaks to the needs of the human heart; that it dispenses a reasonable comfort for the ills and the vicissitudes of human experience, by interpreting them in the light of reason, love, and justice; that, by bringing God into the consciousness, it satisfies the nameless and indescribable longing of the human soul; that it is built on the foundation-rock of prayer- prayer the answer to which is determined not by favoritism, but by an intelligent appropriation of the divine law of supply and demand.

It bases its claim as a science on the fact that it is built on the orderly arrangement of fundamental knowledge- knowledge concerning the laws of cause and effect in human experience; knowledge concerning the creative power of thought; knowledge concerning the laws of attainment, the conditions of accomplishment, the methods of realization and fulfillment; knowledge concerning the principles that underlie the transmutation of undesirable thought environment into desirable; knowledge that seeks practical application not only explaining the

THE SON OF GOD

existing conditions of life but also indicating the laws that make possible the improvement of such conditions.

As a Philosophy, it endeavors to trace first principles in the realms of mind and soul, and to lift the veil that hides from the untrained eye the vital connection between a given effect and its necessitating cause. It clears one's vision regarding what is worth striving after in life. It gives satisfaction in regard to what is the ultimate end and aim of existence. Not to comprehend all knowledge is the criterion of a philosopher; but to love wisdom and to seek wisdom in regard to the vital interests of human experience. Such wisdom constitutes a practical philosophy. When the individual has established in his understanding a reasonably satisfactory philosophy of life, he is free to give all his energy in service to others; for his energies are not distracted and scattered by doubts, fears, and annoyances; his strength and vital forces are not depleted by unnecessary vexation of spirit; his interests and his attention are not divided between this, that, and the other. A philosophy that satisfies, gives to him that holds it peace and poise of mind; thereby he is enabled to give undivided attention to service for others.

In order to understand fundamental principles, it is necessary to explain the meaning of certain terms, and to indicate clearly the content of certain expressions as they are generally used in Illuminati literature. In current writings on religious, psychological, and philosophic subjects, there is more or less confusion in the use of certain words; such as, mind, soul, spirit. Again, there is a dearth of expressions and a need of coining words to express necessary ideas. There is no adjective or noun to denote the attributes of the Individualized Soul, corresponding to the words, spiritual and spirituality; while the words, spiritual and spirituality, are confusing. For, by their derivation, they ought to signify one thing, whereas, in common usage, they are employed to signify something else far removed from their derivative significance. It has been suggested to use the words, soulual and

THE SON OF GOD

souluality, to designate the attributes of the Illumined Soul.

The words, mind, soul, and spirit, are often used loosely; sometimes even interchangeably. General usage has established for each one many different shades of meaning. This affords variety and wealth of expression; but, by this freedom of usage, one who is striving to form a satisfactory correlation of ideas is led to confusion of thought and to inaccuracy of concept. A fine and careful distinction be- tween these words has never become universally established. Different writers and different schools of thought place their own interpretation on these terms. A good way to determine a writer's concept of words is to read all available literature from his pen, and to note by the context their significance. Thus, in time one reaches a satisfactory comprehension of their content as used by that particular writer; also, one gains a sensitive grasp of their significance- a grasp that transcends the niceties of definition. However, it is possible to formulate some important distinctions in regard to this class of words as used in Illuminati literature.

The word, spirit, as herein employed, refers to the breath of life, or to life itself, or to the life-principle. It is common to man, animals, and all animate beings. It is a generic term rather than a specific, or individual; and, as such, it emphasizes the fact that the spirit of man, at the transition state called death, returns to the universal storehouse of spirit, or life, and does not continue its existence as an individuality. Thus, the spirit of man is mortal- mortal as an individualization. To be sure, it is eternal in the sense that its particled elements return to the great universal garner of vital essences ready to be used in other manifestations; it is eternal in the sense that, although all is subject to change and renewal of form, according to the divine economy, nothing really perishes, nothing is lost.

The distinction between mind and soul can best be made by pointing out their relation to each other. To understand this

THE SON OF GOD

relationship at the beginning of one's study, is exceedingly important; for it is fundamental not only in grasping ideas, but particularly in learning to apply these ideas to practical methods of growth. These distinctions are not to be thought of as hard and fast definitions of terms, but rather as various ways of making clear the essential content of terms as used by this school of thought. The purpose is not to define the nomenclature of a science for the mere sake of doing so or for the sake of satisfying a cold, exacting, scientific type of mind, but to make clear to the earnest sincere seeker the content of essential terms, that he may be able to apply the teachings to his own personal needs.

The first distinction to be made is that mind is mortal, while soul is immortal. Mind is mortal as an individualization. Mind is not an entity; it is a fusion of bodily and spiritual elements. It is the connecting link between body, soul, and spirit. It is not wholly of the body, nor is it wholly of the spirit. It is the link between them, the silver cord that binds the three together, and makes manifestation possible.

Again, mind is the creative principle of man's nature, while soul is the receptive principle. Man uses mind as a creating implement, or a creating agency. Through the power of mind, man becomes a creator. In this faculty, he stands alone. The animal is a creator in regard to its own species, but in no other sense. Man is a creator not only in respect to his own species, but in respect to other things as well. He creates character; he creates thought environment; in large measure, he has created the conditions by which his life is surrounded. In large measure, he has the ability to change conditions, the ability to improve them if he will. This ability to alter, to transform, to improve, is one aspect of his creative tendencies. The Soul, being the receptive principle of man's nature, is the storehouse, or the receptacle, or the resultant, of that which his mind creates.

When man realizes that the soul is the result of his own

THE SON OF GOD

creation, and that it partakes of the nature of his own creative thought, he will learn to be careful what thoughts and what moods he allows in his life. More than this, he will see that it is necessary to put forth conscious, deliberate effort, and to give himself effective training, in order that the creations of his mind may be pure, holy, and worthy. In time, he will come to be actuated by one desire, namely; the desire to create no thought image and to mold no thought form except that which is in harmony with the love, truth, and justice of the Christ Ideal.

Another way of expressing the relation between mind and soul is to regard mind as the realm of causation; while soul is the result of causation, or the accumulation of that which mind has caused. Man's thought kingdom is his Cause World. His thoughts have power to produce changes, to bring about results, to affect conditions, to create environment. The wise man voiced this law when he said: "A merry heart doeth good like a medicine." Each one knows in his own experience how true it is that he accomplishes more when his mind- his cause world- is tempered by the atmosphere of peace, poise, and composure.

When man realizes that the soul is the result of his own causation and that its character corresponds to the type of influences he allows in his own thought kingdom, he will become active and earnest in securing masterful control in his realm of causes. To be able to take one's place on the throne of the cause world and to issue and execute such decrees as are in harmony with the love, truth, and justice of the Christ Character- to be able to do this will become his highest ambition. To this end he will put forth every effort; he will give to his will-power a rigorous course of training; to his desire nature he will apply every plausible means of cleansing and purifying; his understanding he will subject to patient instruction in the principles of love, truth, and justice.

Sacred literature is replete with figures which illustrate,

THE SON OF GOD

from different points of view, the creative, or active, principle of mind, and the receptive, or passive, principle of soul. A favorite figure among all nations represents mind as the builder, or the architect, and Soul as the temple of character that is builded by the power of mind. In this building process, mind takes the initiative; mind executes choices, selects material, rejects material, according to its own judgment; mind makes decisions and executes willpower. The builder may pass away, or return whence it came; but the temple stands as a living testimony to the desires, the choices, the decisions, the imaginations, the thoughts, that the architect permitted to enter as building-material into his structure.

When man realizes that the soul is the result of his own building, that the edifice of character is the result of the mind's selecting, rejecting, and executing, he will spare no pains in giving himself such training as a Master Architect needs.

Man is made in the image of God. He is a reflection of the Infinite, possessing the powers and the attributes of the Infinite. In different beings, these divine qualities are in different stages of unfoldment. In one, they may be in a latent state, concealed from view beneath the crust of a selfish personality; but, unless they have been burned and seared by the fire of persistent wrong doing, they are none the less a potentiality, awaiting the unfolding processes of growth. In another, they may be in the incipient stages of. a nucleus of goodness. In this state, they indicate an active, wholesome conscience; although the life may be pain- fully entangled and fettered and hampered by the lower personality. Yet, again, these qualities may have become a dynamic, vital expression of individualized life, such that the soul is conscious of its inseparable connection with the Infinite. They may have condensed into a center of radiation, into a perfect, pyramidal flame that warms the desire nature with love, and illumines the understanding with truth. In this state, the divine qualities of love, truth, and justice unconsciously radiate, to those with whom the life comes in contact, the blessings of their inherent goodness.

THE SON OF GOD

Creation is the manifestation of the Divine Mind. All things, having been created by God, are, in themselves, good; but, through free-will, man may pervert the good by wrong use, and thus cause evil; he may misdirect possibilities that are inherently blessed, and thus bring on himself and others a painful curse.

In his fourfold nature, body, mind, spirit, and soul, man is an epitome of the universe. Potentially, he is the divine creation in miniature, and, consequently, has been called the microcosm, or little world. He is the climax and the culmination of forces, which for ages have been seeking expression. How to use his forces and to express them harmoniously, is the problem placed before him. To use them in harmony with the Divine Law and the divine purpose and to express them only in service to mankind- this is the ideal he must be led to understand and to choose for himself. To use his powers and his possibilities in obedience to the law of goodness and in keeping with the correct understanding of truth, leads to good. To pervert his powers and to misdirect his inherent possibilities in channels of error and sin, result in evil.

God has placed no higher mark of honor on man than to give him the right of choice, the power of decision, and the ability to direct will-power and to execute plans in accordance with his own decree. Every power, is, in itself, good, although it admits of a twofold expression, positive and negative. Every law of his nature is, in itself, good, although it admits of a twofold functioning, constructive and upbuilding or destructive and disintegrating. The use one makes of a law determines its effect. Every virtue admits of a corresponding vice. Results depend on the use given to power, on the direction that a tendency takes. Every force, every possibility, placed within man's reach is intended to serve a certain noble purpose. When used in harmony with the law of its highest purpose, the result is good. When perverted or misused, the results are evil. It is time for man to understand that he is individually responsible for putting forth intelligent effort to understand the laws of his own being and to

THE SON OF GOD

obey their highest call. One distinctive aim of the Temple of Illumination is to give clear instructions concerning the laws of right and justice in order that man may intelligently choose his steps, and know how to cultivate his manifold powers and to direct them in proper channels.

Christic Interpretation and Mystic Christianity, as herein outlined, are not a teaching separate and distinct from the lessons as taught in Soul Science, but form a part of these teachings. The books, "Christic Interpretation of St. Matthew," "The Illuminated Faith of St. John," and "The Son of God," as well as "Christisis" give these teachings in full and are a part of the courses of study given in the various departments of the Illuminati.

However, it is not necessary for one to take the instructions in Soul Science. But simply to secure and read the text-books as outlined herein, entitles one to membership in the Temple of Illumination. In order to belong to the Temple of the Illuminati, which is the inner circle, it is necessary to enroll for the course of lessons in Soul Science, and to secure the text-books that are included in this course of study.

The seeker after truth should bear in mind that any of these books may be bought separately and without obligation on his part to join either the Temple of Illuminati or the Temple of Illumination. Membership is optional on the part of students, and is for those who desire fellowship with others who are seeking the truth, and for those who understand that only in unity can the greatest amount of good be accomplished.

THE END

Made in the USA
Columbia, SC
20 April 2025